# George Allen's
## *New*
# HANDBOOK OF
# FOOTBALL DRILLS

*George Allen*

**PRENTICE-HALL, INC.** *Englewood Cliffs, N.J.*

Prentice-Hall International, Inc., *London*
Prentice-Hall of Australia, Pty. Ltd., *Sydney*
Prentice-Hall of Canada, Ltd., *Toronto*
Prentice-Hall of India, Private Ltd., *New Delhi*
Prentice-Hall of Japan, Inc., *Tokyo*

Third Printing . . . . . August, 1975

**Library of Congress Cataloging in Publication Data**

Allen, George Herbert,
    George Allen's new handbook of football drills.

    1.  Football.  I.  Title.  II.  Title: Handbook
of football drills.
GV951.A682          796.33'2                73-19668
ISBN 0-13-352716-6

Printed in the United States of America

*to my three sons,*
*George, Gregory, and Bruce*
*of whom I am very proud*

# WHAT'S IN THIS BOOK FOR YOU

Since my *Complete Book of Winning Football Drills* was published in 1959, the game of football has changed radically. Although the passing game has undergone the most dramatic changes, every other phase of football, offensive and defensive, has been refined and upgraded. Even though my book continued to sell exceptionally well, going through 14 printings, I realized that a new book was needed covering all aspects of football drills which would be relevant to today's exciting game.

Every coach has an encyclopedia of drills, some of which possibly date back to Knute Rockne's time, and some of these drills are still valuable. However, I believe there is a definite need for every coach, regardless of his experience or the level of football he is coaching, to update his repertoire of drills to keep pace with the latest trends.

*George Allen's* New *Handbook of Football Drills* covers the entire game of football from the opening kick-off to the final whistle. This new book presents more than 300 drills for teaching every phase of football. Many time-tested drills which have been perfected over the years have been modernized and made applicable to today's game. I have also introduced many brand-new drills, in addition to presenting new ideas for using old drills. In short, this book provides an up-to-date catalog of the most useful and successful drills available to coaches today.

The reader will find drills for the Veer and Wishbone offenses and defenses which have been employed with increasing regularity and success at both the high school and college levels. Another feature of this New Handbook is the very latest in drilling methods as practiced by the pros. These include drills to improve both the offensive and defensive facets of the passing game which has become more and more intricate each season. The kicking game, which increasingly spells the difference between victory and defeat, is discussed in depth. This book covers every possible drill situation from A to Z through the use of over 200 illustrations and diagrams.

The organization of this book ranges from the very basics of individual football instruction to the complex coordination of team play. Each phase starts with the first steps, positions and moves that every player must take regardless of his offensive or defensive position, and progresses to skilled individual drills. The next phase features drills for semi-groups in which players are drilled to interact with nearby teammates. This is followed by drills for groups where segments of a team are taught to meet situations. Finally there are valuable team drills where every conceivable game possibility is mastered.

Since agility, conditioning and reaction are factors which play such an important part in the development of players, and therefore, the success of teams, I have devoted a section of this book to drills that will improve these areas. There is also a section providing drills to be performed indoors for those situations when outdoor practice is not possible.

As an added feature, I have presented what I consider to be the top ten drills of the last decade and my reasoning for including each. These are, in my opinion, the most proven ten drills used today.

If you coach football, regardless of your experience, at any level from little leagues to the pros, you'll find a vast storehouse of valuable teaching methods contained in this volume.

**GEORGE ALLEN**

# CONTENTS

# 1
# HOW TO COACH DRILLS

## A. BASIC FUNDAMENTALS TO ALL DRILLS

A practice program is no better than the drills that go to make it up. The secret then to successful performance is a well planned drill organization.

Some football coaches have fallen into the trap of drilling just for the sake of drilling. A drill must have a reason beyond that of the drill itself. To explain further, let's look at the different kinds of drills:

### 1. SKILL DRILLS

These drills are important to teach the "tools of the trade." Individuals must master the basic techniques of the position they play. There is no interaction in these drills; they simply improve personal skill. This type of drill trains the motor response, but the motor response must be in relation to the goals of the trainee.

### 2. CONDITIONING DRILLS

There are some drills whose sole purpose is to prepare the body to withstand increasing physical activity. These drills must be carefully selected or the coach may waste valuable time. Wherever possible, the conditioning drill should also teach the job to be done. There should be a "carryover" factor in all conditioning drills.

### 3. SITUATION DRILLS

These drills are the most important drills in football. Here is where the athlete really learns to play his position. These are game situations and are exactly what he'll be faced with throughout the contest. If you don't have a heavy dose of these drills in your practice schedule, you will eventually pay the penalty of poor execution.

### 4. INTERACTION DRILLS

Here is where the team member learns to function as a member of a unit. You simply cannot time out a trap play without the center, the power block, the trapper, the quarterback, and the ballcarrier all working together. On defense, you cannot teach combination zone coverage without the interplay of the defenders.

### 5. TEAM DRILLS

This is where the coach puts it all together. It is vital but should not dominate the practice schedule. Probably the biggest mistake that is made in practice schedules is devoting too much time to team execution.

### 6. MISCELLANEOUS DRILLS

These drills serve a necessary funtion but should be kept in their place. Such things as warmup drills, mental drills, morale drills and agility drills are useful but should be scheduled carefully.

This is a quick rundown of the types of drills. The reason behind the drill is still the most important feature of drilling. A coaching staff must plan the practice schedule with drills that accomplish as many things at one time, or within one drill, as possible. This is what is meant by having a reason for a drill. For example, conditioning, alignment, agility and keying can all be coordinated into one drill. Another example is windsprints. Windsprints are necessary, but there is no reason why they can't be accomplished by running dummy plays, with 11 men, sprinting from hash mark to sideline and then turning around immediately and running back to the hashmark. Now you are not only getting the conditioning but the alignments, starting cadence and ball-handling at the same time. Another way to combine sprints is to break into small groups, each with a quarterback, and throw the long bomb to each individual. Linemen will get in a number of 50-yard sprints and will develop some ability to catch while the quarterbacks are practicing the long pass.

The main reason for drilling has to be development of weak areas. Many coaches will say all areas are weak on their particular team, but certainly one or two areas are the weakest. These should become emphasis areas. Drills must also accomplish the goal of teaching the team's offensive and defensive plan. This book will cover drills of all kinds but it is set up in such a way that it resembles a practice plan in itself. The first drills covered will be individual drills. From there the natural progression to semi-group drills, on to group drills, and finally ending with team drills. This is the building processing in each practice session.

1. Individual  —Skill Drills
2. Semi-Group  —Situation Drills
3. Group  —Interact Drills
4. Team  —Put It All Together Drills

## B. WHEN, WHERE AND HOW TO USE DRILLS

When to use drills? Actually the whole spectrum of practice is nothing but a series of drills; so a team drills all the time. Here is a general list on when to use certain types of drills.

| EVERYDAY | EASY DAYS | WORK DAYS |
|---|---|---|
| Warmup drills | Warmup drills | Warmup drills |
| Agility drills | Agility drills | Agility drills |
| Individual drills | Dummy reaction drills | Individual hitting |
| Situation drills | Dummy situation drills | Situation hitting |
| Group drills | Dummy group drills | Group hitting |
| Team drills | Dummy team drills | Goal line hitting |
| Kicking drills | Kickers only drills | Full speed kicking |
| | | Scrimmage |

Another factor involved in when to use certain drills is the monotony of routine. If a coach uses the same drills at the same time every day he may gain some benefits due to repetition, but he may also lose mental motivation. There must be enough spice in the practice routine to keep the interest of the players.

Again, the "when" of drills is dictated by need. As mentioned before, weak areas must receive the emphasis treatment. After the first scrimmage in the fall, your drill program should be altered to allow you to concentrate on those areas that are most in need of refinement.

*Where to use drills* is a mechanical process of dividing field space in the most logical manner. Let's examine the needs of the various groups within the team.

### 1. OFFENSIVE LINE

The offensive line group always has more mechanical devices and training equipment than any other group. Therefore, they should be assigned an area that can support the paraphernalia. Such things as the sleds, the shoots, the planks, the heavy bag, and other types of training aids need space. Also, they must be far enough off the marked field so as not to be a hazard. Beyond the end zone area in one corner of the practice perimeter is usually the logical spot.

### 2. OFFENSIVE BACKS AND RECEIVERS

This group should always drill in a marked area. The hash marks and boundaries are most necessary. Their logical place is from the 40-yard line on into the end zone on the end of the field closest to the offensive line.

### 3. DEFENSIVE BACKS

This group also needs the markings; therefore, they should be assigned the other half of the field from the offensive backs and receivers.

### 4. DEFENSIVE LINE

This group should be behind the end zone the defensive backs are defending. Their equipment and field markings should be in this area.

## 5. DEFENSIVE LINEBACKERS

This group needs a small personal drilling area but they swing a good deal, alternating with the line and backs. Because of this, they should be along the defensive end of the field, just off the sidelines.

## 6. MISCELLANEOUS AREA

The remaining area, opposite the offensive line area, should include such equipment that is used by both offensive and defensive units, such as the ropes and other agility and conditioning equipment.

Here is a sample diagram showing drill areas based on the premise there is only one fully marked football field.

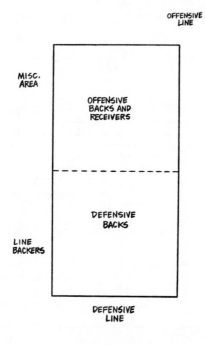

DIAGRAM #1

*How to use drills* (ten rules of thumb)

1. Never more than 20 minutes per drill
2. Don't sap the players' vitality on any one drill

3. Keep the element of fun present
4. Space the hard-hitting drills with slower-paced drills
5. Keep individuality present in all drills
6. Don't keep ten players waiting while you spend a dispropor-tionate amount of time with one player
7. Correct in a positive manner. Use the expression, "Do it this way." Do not use the expression, "Don't do it that way."
8. Plan your work, work your plan
9. Encourage the players to set the tempo. The coach should not dominate the drill
10. There is no substitute for enthusiasm

### How to organize a practice schedule

Offensive and Defensive coaches must sit down together every day and plan the schedule. Practice schedule forms should be printed up before the season and filled out daily during this meeting. Diagram #2 is a sample blank form:

| | | | | | | |
|---|---|---|---|---|---|---|
| | | | | | | |

| DEFENSIVE PRACTICE SCHEDULE | | | | | | 3 SEPT '73 |
|---|---|---|---|---|---|---|
| SCHEDULE | | | TIME | REQUIREMENTS | | |
| BACKS | LINEBACKER | LINE | | BACKS | LINEBACKERS | LINE |
| | | | | | | |
| | | | | | | |
| | | | | | | |
| | | | | | | |
| | | | | | | |
| | | | | | | |

**DIAGRAM #2**

This form can be used for the longest practice sessions and the shortest. Diagrams #3 and #4 are examples of each after being completed.

| DEFENSIVE PRACTICE SCHEDULE | | | | 3 SEPT. '73 | | |
|---|---|---|---|---|---|---|
| SCHEDULE | | | TIME | REQUIREMENTS | | |
| BACKS | LINEBACKERS | LINE | | BACKS | LINEBACKERS | LINE |
| SPECIALTY | POSTS | POSTS | 345 400 | | | |
| INDIVIDUAL | INDIVIDUAL | INDIVIDUAL | 400 420 | SKELETON OFF. | 7 BODIES | OFF. LINE + ONE QB |
| SEMI GROUP | SEMI GROUP | SEMI GROUP | 420 440 | SAME | ONE QB | SAME |
| B R E A K | | | 440 405 | | | |
| GROUP | WITH LINE | GROUP | 445 505 | PASSER + RECEIVER | | ONE TEAM |
| PERIMITER | ALTERNATE | PERIMITER | 505 545 | TWO BACKFIELDS + RECEIVERS | | ONE TEAM |
| TEAM | TEAM | TEAM | 545 605 | ALTERNATING TEAMS | | |
| COUNTY FAIR | COUNTY FAIR | COUNTY FAIR | 605 615 | | | |

DIAGRAM #3

| DEFENSIVE PRACTICE SCHEDULE | | | | 7 SEPT. '73 | | |
|---|---|---|---|---|---|---|
| SCHEDULE | | | TIME | REQUIREMENTS | | |
| BACKS | LINEBACKERS | LINE | | BACKS | LINEBACKERS | LINE |
| WARM UP | WARM UP | WARM UP | 400 405 | | | |
| INDIVIDUAL | INDIVIDUAL | INDIVIDUAL | 405 415 | | | |
| PERIMETER | | PERIMETER | 415 445 | ONE | TEAM | |
| B R E A K | | | 445 450 | | | |
| TEAM | TEAM | TEAM | 450 530 | TWO | TEAMS | |
| | | | | | | |
| | | | | | | |

DIAGRAM #4

You will notice that the B Team or junior varsity coaches are informed as to when and where their people are needed by the varsity.

Each coach should keep a personal time card showing the time spent on different phases of the game. This always helps in planning future practices. Diagram #5 shows such a form.

| | NO. OF MINUTES SPENT ON EACH ACTIVITY | | |
|---|---|---|---|
| | 1ST WEEK | 2ND WEEK | TOTAL |
| DATE | | | |
| CONDITIONING | | | |
| FILMS | | | |
| MEETING | | | |
| AGILITY | | | |
| REACTION | | | |
| KEYING | | | |
| PURSUIT | | | |
| TACKLING | | | |
| SEMI GP. | | | |
| GROUP | | | |
| TEAM | | | |
| RULES | | | |
| | | | |
| | | | |

DIAGRAM #5

# C. PRACTICE ORGANIZATION WITH EMPHASIS ON DRILLS

## 1. EARLY SEASON AND TWO-A-DAY

A general rule here is that the morning practice should be 1½ hours long and the afternoon practice about two hours. (This does not include pre- and post-practice drills.)

Pre-practice drills are often called Specialty Periods. They usually last about 15 minutes after a brief stretching and loosening warm up.

a. Punters and one of the rotating centers work from mid-field towards one goal. The kicker should be at a distance where his punts will fall right around the 10-yard line.

b. Punt receivers work on the catch in the 10-yard area. Since this is the most difficult area in which to receive punts, always practice here.

c. Extra-point and field-goal kickers and holders work with one of the alternating centers at the opposite goal. Managers can shag these kicks.

d. Kickoff men must work the sideline with kickoff receivers catching them and running them back.

e. Passers and receivers play easy catch.

f. Informality is the key to the rest of the team. Coaches encourage a work on individual weaknesses. This is also a good time for isometric exercises for the bigger and stronger linemen.

A horn or whistle should sound the beginning of organized practice. The next step is team warmups. This should be done with everybody in one group. It is one of the few times both offense and defense are actually together. The drill should be six to eight minutes long and very snappy. The object is not entirely conditioning but mental preparation as well. This sort of sets the tempo. Such well-proven exercises as side-straddle-hop, toe tapper, windmill and burpees are good group exercises. Certain positions on the team require different warmups. It is a good ideas to do these immediately after the team warmups. As soon as the short team warmup ends, each group should hustle to their areas for special warmups peculiar to those positions. Examples:

*Defensive backs and linebackers.* Because of the quick changing of direction demanded by their position, they should do all the exercises that stretch groin and hamstring muscles.

*Defensive linemen.* Perform extensive drills in flipper and shiver exercises, pushups, etc.

*Offensive backs and receivers.* These people should concentrate on long striding and crossover exercises.

*Offensive linemen.* Do neck bridges, leg thrusts, rocking chair, etc.

At this stage of the season there are certain conditioning exercises and agility drills that every position should do. To conserve time but make sure a wide range of these drills is accomplished, a good method is the rotating stations or county fair method of drilling. The idea is to start by dividing the team into six or seven groups—one at each station. The drill at each station should take no longer than two or three minutes. Of course, it follows that the groups rotate until all have visited each station. Here is a sample of what each station does.

*Station #1: Ropes.* Once through alternating slots—once through sideways—once through crossing over.

*Station #2: Wave drills.* Right, left, forwards, back, up and down on sight signals. Coach uses football to give direction.

*Station #3: Quick arounds.* Players sprint forward and "quick around" in a circle using down hand for balance.

*Station #4: Backward and sideways running drills.* There are many of these such as the grapevine (run sideways, alternating the trailing leg in front and then in back of the leading leg), and switch running (running backward and turning body to right and left sides without turning back on coach).

*Station #5: Tumbling.* Example is three men doing the over and roll. By constantly rolling then jumping back over man rolling to you, you can keep the three men rolling and jumping.

*Station #6: Zig-zag running.* Player runs across the football field starting on one sideline. He runs at a 45° angle to the next 5-yard line; here he plants his inside foot and makes an inside pivot and runs at a 45° angle back to the 5-yard stripe he started on. This continues in a zig-zag fashion until he crosses the field.

After this county fair drill, the next item on the practice schedule is individual drills. The time allotted is usually 20 minutes. The players go immediately to their assigned areas and report to their particular coach. All of the skill drills used to train the individual are described in detail throughout this book. Since we are dealing in this chapter with types of drills in relation to practice organization during early season and two-a-day (two sessions in one day), the actual drills will come up later.

Individual drills during two-a-day should encompass a lot of hitting from close range. Even if the morning workout is in shorts, shoulder pads and headgear should be worn so limited hitting can take place. This is necessary to build up the body for football. Development of the football body is different from, for example, development of the swimmer's body. A toughening must take place so that a high degree of bruise resistance will develop. If the player has done a reasonable job of pre-practice summer training, he should be able to start hitting the first day. After three days of two-a-day with hitting, he will reach his maximum soreness. After this passes, his body should be able to withstand all the normal blows of practice or game. Along with hitting, his conditioning should include a lot of running. Of course this develops the legs and wind and is most essential. Individual drills during two-a-day should be longer, since getting into shape is of prime importance. You may have to borrow time from group and team drills at this early stage; then as the first game nears, the reverse is true.

After individual drills come the semi-group drills, which are situation drills. This is where you teach the player how to play his position. These drills can be half-speed or full-speed. In high school, a great deal of time should be spent in these drills because this is where the fundamentals are learned. It is better to have a simple offensive and defensive plan (which requires less time) and spend more time on fundamentals. It is the exceptional high school team that can run a wide variety of patterns and still be sound fundamentally; in fact, it is rather exceptional in college football. These situation drills should always put the player in game-type situations. For example, a coach says, "All right boys, today we are going to tackle." They then proceed to whack away at each other. This is not a game-type situation. The proper way is to align the player in his proper alignment, give him a blocker to key or ward off, and then tackle a back carrying the football by proper positioning, leverage or pursuit. You will notice I said a "back" carrying the ball. Linemen should not tackle other linemen.

At this point I'd like to interject the following thought. All assistant coaches should carry a whistle to be consistent with game-type situations. Since a whistle stops the play in football, all drills should be controlled the same way.

Next, during two-a-day, are the group drills. These drills require careful planning since they are based on interaction and, if the people you are working against don't know what they are doing, your drill will fail. Here is where the overall plan takes shape. Within the plan, each group learns how to fit the different responsibilities together. During two-a-days, there should be considerable live or full-speed action. After the season starts, the place should continue full-speed but tackling should be eliminated. You lose timing if you do these drills half-speed. Eliminating tackling prevents pileups and reduces the possibility of injury. It is very hard to control a full-speed dummy drill, but it can be done.

Finally, the team drills usually conclude the practice. You must make time for the team kicking game in this period. A good way to make sure it gets its proper time (10 to 15 percent of all the plays in a football game are kicking plays) is to keep moving the line of scrimmage up and down the field. After the goal area is covered, kick the extra point, then back up and kick a field goal. Turn the offense around and declare fourth down. Execute the punt (or punt return if working on defense—or both if scrimmaging). After practice, cover kickoffs as a substitute for windsprints. Kickoff coverage and kickoff returns can also be fit in the schedule right after the County Fair.

Post-practice drills are usually conditioning drills. At this stage of the season the player should be nearly exhausted when he leaves the field.

While we are still on the subject of early-season practice, it should be mentioned that in extremely hot weather, liquid breaks should occur two or three times in the practice schedule. As the weather cools off, the breaks can be reduced to one or two.

## 2. EARLY-SEASON SCRIMMAGE ORGANIZATION

At first, the units within your team cannot scrimmage for long periods of time without breaks. It is also the time you wish to get a look at some of the squad men all the way down the line. It will help the organization of your scrimmage if you use a variety of contrasting colors on your different units. Since it is highly desirable to film these scrimmages, you should have numbers on every player. Here is a sample color breakdown:

First and second offensive teams—*white with dark numbers*
First and second defensive teams—*blue with white numbers*

First and second B team offense—*red with white numbers*
First and second B team defense —*orange with white numbers*
First and second Frosh offense —*green with white numbers*
First and second Frosh defense —*yellow with dark numbers*

Actually, it is highly desirable to dress them this way every practice. You may wish to alternate colors between your varsity offense and defense since you will play in both your dark and light jerseys. After the season starts, if your squad is big enough, both offense and defense will suit up in the color of the week. If not, you'll have to wear contrasting colors so the offense and defense can work against each other.

By using the color scheme outlined above, the scrimmage can be planned this way:

| | |
|---|---|
| First off vs. first B def | 15 plays |
| First def vs. first B off | 15 plays |
| Second off vs. second B def | 15 plays |
| Second def vs. second B off | 15 plays |
| First off vs. second def | 15 plays |
| Second off vs. first def | 15 plays |
| First frosh off vs. first B def | 15 plays |
| First frosh def vs. first B off | 15 plays |
| First off vs. first def | 15 plays |
| Second off vs. second def | 15 plays |
| Second frosh off vs. second B def | 15 plays |
| Second frosh def vs. second B off | 15 plays |

This organization assumes that you have 132 players dressed out. Very few squads are actually that large; however, early season finds many tryouts and the first scrimmage should give you a look at every kid. On the average you will have three full-scale game-type scrimmages before the first game. After the first one, your squad will thin out. Injuries and disenchantment will set in. The next two game-type scrimmages will concentrate more on your top two offenses and defenses. There is one determining factor here. The frosh offense cannot put on a good offensive picture at least until the season starts; therefore, the B Team must stack their offense. The Frosh can usually do a pretty good job of presenting a defensive picture. So if you get really thin in numbers, it usually boils down to the B Team versus the varsity defense and the frosh versus the varsity offense.

### 3. MONDAY PRACTICE

This subtitle assumes that the game is to be on Saturday. If you play Friday, it's Sunday practice, and if you play Sunday, it's Tuesday practice. These practices are usually in sweats and they stress working out the soreness. This means a heavy dose of running and agility drills. There are no individual drills, limited situation drills, limited group, a long team period to correct errors in the last game, and start the game plan for next week. The kicking game should get a lot of attention. The reason you can't get entirely into the game plan is because there are usually several key players still not able to do much, and because after you fool around with the plan on Monday, some things will come up you haven't thought of. This gives you a chance to work out the kinks and be set to go for real the next day.

### 4. WORK DAY PRACTICES

During the season you have two work days to put in the plan. You should use the full practice schedule:

- Warmup
- KO cover and receive
- Individual
- Semi-group
- Group
- Team
- Team kicking
- Conditioning

You should continue to drill on fundamentals during the individual, semi-group, and group drills, but team drills must include both the fundamentals and the special plan for the week. Therefore, you must give a lot of time to this. The bare minimum to get both offensive teams and both defensive teams ready to play is one hour. The best way to split this up is to have both the first and second offenses going against the next opponent's defenses at the same time on one field, back-to-back.

Another way to keep two offensive units going at once is to have two huddles facing one defense in shields or aprons. The offensive teams alternate plays. By having one offense calling a play while the other is running a play, the time element is about the same as if just one team were running plays. Of course, the defense has to hustle to alignments quickly. These drills will be described in detail under team drills later on in this book.

The defense can work the perimeter against the opponent's offense on one half of a field while the line can work against another unit at the same time. All that is required is to swap linebackers. The perimeter works against the pass 75%, run 25%, while the line reverses the emphasis. This gets the most people ready at the same time; however, there is still value in allotting time to one unit working alone, with all the coaches hootin' and hollerin' and the second unit on the sideline.

## 5. LAST PRACTICE BEFORE THE GAME

There is probably more variety in the approach to this day than in any other type of practice. It depends on the philosophy of the head coach. Some coaches take a very grim, businesslike approach to this day. To them, there is never enough time to cover all eventualities and every minute must be productive. The game plan must be perfected and polished in this "dress rehearsal." Nonsense cannot be tolerated. Many of these coaches are big winners. The opposite end of this philosophy also has its devotees. The coaches who go this route feel like all the hard work has been done: the "hay is in the barn" approach. The players have been commanded to view films, work on the plan, pay the practice price, and now it's just a matter of review. This philosophy takes into account the fact that there should be one day when the pressure is off. They feel that kids are kids and that they should have some fun and a release from the grind by various forms of nonsense. Well, this is the day to do it. The coaches allow the players to wear goofy hats or uniform variances and kid around a lot. They still review the plan but in a very light manner. I am not going to be a strong advocate for either approach, except to say that I think either can be overdone. It is an absolute must that every player go through what is expected of him on game day. The kicking game must be covered in its entirety. Here is a sample of the type of schedule needed:

1. Warmup
2. 10 minutes individual
3. 10 minutes group
4. 40 minutes offense and defense, up and down the field
   a. Advance the ball 5 yards each play going from hash to middle to hash
   b. Use chains and down markers

   c. Use a pre-written script to set the situations
   d. Cover all goal-line situations
   e. Cover all kicking situations
   f. Kickoff and receive
   g. Cover the checklist of oddball situations: such things as
      safties, rules, late in the half or game, injuries and adjust-
      ments (especially to specialists such as punt receivers), ex-
      tremes in weather, rainy day defenses
   h. Bench organization
   i. Before first game, the pre-game warmup must be rehearsed

## 6. PRE-GAME PRACTICE

   Weather conditions dictate the length of the pre-game practice.
Cold weather demands a longer warmup than does extremely hot
weather. Certain things should be done regardless of the weather.
Kickers have to kick, passers have to pass, receivers have to catch,
backs must handle the ball, and everyone should stretch and take a few
blows. This is no time to frantically review the game plan. A few
reminders are ok. Also this is no time for a conditioning drill. Before
leaving the dressing room, the field division for warmup should be
drawn on the blackboard. Here is a sample schedule, assuming a 2:00
p.m. kickoff.

**1:25**   Specialists, kickers and receivers take the field and
         warm up together for 5 minutes.

**1:30**   Punters and center kick to punt receivers both with
         and against the wind. Center alternates with centers
         working with field-goal group. Field-goal kickers,
         holders and center work into goal assigned for this
         drill. Passers and receivers run basic patterns. Kick-
         off men kick both ways using sideline area.

**1:35**   Linemen and remaining players leave dressing room
         for warmup.

**1:40**   Second group breaks into groups. Defensive secon-
         dary people catch. Linemen start and get a few good
         shoulder pops. Specialists should be through now
         and join their groups. A few drills may be used by

the different groups. Various reaction drills are good, such as wave drills, facing drills, tip drills, etc.

**1:50**  Defensive teams leave the field and offensive teams get off on the cadence a few times and follow defense off the field by a few minutes.

**1:53**  Perspiration, elimination, inspiration.

**1:57**  Take the field.

## 7. HALFTIME WARMUP

Some coaches favor group exercises and this is ok. Use a couple of normal sidestraddles, windmills, and toe tappers. Personally, I feel that each player should informally stretch the key muscles, get a few starts and take a couple of shoulder pops. Stretching is the most important thing. Every player with experience will do this because he knows he could pull a muscle if not loosened up. High schoolers get so excited they frequently forget to do this. That is why you'll see more formal warmups at high school games and less as the players mature.

# 2

# INDIVIDUAL OFFENSIVE DRILLS

## A. CENTERS

### 1. DRILL FOR THE STANCE

Have all the center candidates line up on a yard line across the field. Each center has a ball in front of him with the end of the ball on the yard stripe.

DIAGRAM #6

Together, the centers go through the following steps to a good stance. This is similar to a soldier learning the manual of arms by the numbers.

a. Feet apart, slightly wider than the shoulders. Long-legged centers can spread a little wider.

b. Stagger the right foot back. For short-legged men, it should be even with the instep of the up foot. Average leg length is back an inch or so farther. The long-legged center may stagger his right foot back even with the heel of the left foot. A general rule is: the shorter the legs, the less the stagger; the longer the legs, the greater the stagger.

   c. Heels slightly to the outside. This produces a slight pigeon-toed stance for balance.

   d. Elbows on knees.

   e. Lean forward and grasp ball. Head should be almost over the forward point of the ball. (Laces on the ball should be straight up.) The right hand should grip the ball as far forward as possible and still achieve a good firm grip. This is the same grip the quarterback uses in throwing the ball. The left hand is around the middle of the ball and most of the weight is placed on this hand. The laces of the ball should pass under the area between the thumb and forefinger. The forefinger should point straight down. Of course, this is the two-handed grip, which we favor. Many coaches teach the one-handed grip with the left hand down on the ground the same as the rest of the linemen. This one-handed grip must be further back on the ball. We feel the exchange with the quarterback is more consistent with the two-handed grip. In either case, the rear of the ball should be tilted up slightly.

   f. Delivery. The ball is delivered to the middle of the crotch by a pendulum swing of the right arm and a quarter turn of the wrist. This should place the laces of the ball on the quarterback's fingers. The quarterback is responsible for placing the back of his throwing hand, fingers extended to their fullest, hard against the middle of the center's crotch. It is imperative that he always place his hand in the same place and apply lifting pressure with the back of his hand.

   g. Forward step. Just as the center's arm is making the pendulum swing, his right (back) foot is starting to drive forward. It should be in motion when the ball hits the quarterback's hand. Arm, then foot. Never allow the center to pass the ball to the quarterback without this forward motion. This is true even if the center is going to drop back and pass block.

## 2. DRILL FOR THE EXCHANGE

Use the same setup as drilling for stance but add a quarterback to each center and a long bag and holder in front of the ball. Always have someone on the center's nose in every drill you do.

a. Have one quarterback bark the starting signal.
b. All centers deliver the ball to their quarterbacks on the count.
c. Centers drive into bag.
d. Quarterbacks rotate calling the cadence.
e. Quarterbacks rotate to different centers. Do not let one quarterback and one center work together *all* the time.

## 3. DRILLS FOR STARTING

Starting is most important for the offensive line. This usually encompasses the entire line. A good line of scrimmage gets off together like greyhounds coming out of the starting box.

Take a quarterback and a full line and work on getting off precisely together. These drills can be done in the following ways:

a. Against the wind
b. Coming out of shoots which teach spacing and driving out low
c. Using a beveled 2″ x 12″ plank in front of each lineman to assure a wide base.
d. Starting into the seven-man charging sled
e. Starting into shields, bags or aprons

## 4. DRILLS FOR FIREOUT BLOCKS

This style of blocking requires the blocker to drive directly into the middle of an opponent. It eliminates keying or head-reading by the defender, but should be accompanied by good faking in the backfield. Since bags or sleds aren't realistic, drilling for this block should be done against a man or a man in a blocking apron.

### *One-on-one drill*

Place a defender over the ball, on or off the line of scrimmage. Have a quarterback give the cadence and take the ball. Center makes exchange and tries to drive the defender straight back. Confine the defender to an area two paces wide by using towels, flat shields or long dummies laid down.

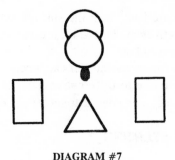

DIAGRAM #7

### Butt 'em and stay with 'em drill

Use the same idea as one-on-one, except eliminate the confining area. This is a slow-whistle drill. On the snap, the center executes the fireout block. He may or may not drive the defender back. The defender must keep coming square at the blocker. The blocker must keep butting at the defender. This goes on for an unrealistic amount of time. While this drill is somewhat unrelated to actual game conditions, it teaches some valuable points. First, the basis of the wishbone, drive, or split-T type of running attack is for the offensive line to maintain contact throughout the play and take stunting linemen the way they want to go. Another value is in building the competitive spirit of your linemen. Dogged determination to stay with blocks can be inculcated with this type of drill. Sooner or later the fighter will win this drill. The less determined may win the first pop, but his sticktoitiveness may fade. Since this is a very exhausting drill, it should be followed by a slower-paced drill.

### Special sled drill

If fireout blocks are the main part of your offense, you should have a one-man sled with the two vertical uprights just wide enough apart for the blocker to put his head between. You will still need the quarterback to take the exchange.

### One-on-one on the plank

Use a plank or board ten feet long, 2" x 12" with beveled edges. Have your center and quarterback align at the end of the plank. This drill can be done live or dummy. If dummy, use a stand-up bag and holder. If alive, simply execute the one-on-one drill on the plank. This forces the center to keep a wide base and not to cant (or turn) his back.

It is impossible to drive down the length of the plank unless the blocker keeps his shoulders square, because if he turns his back and shoulders, his feet will have to come together. This means he'll hit the plank and lose his footing.

DIAGRAM #8

## 5. DRILLS FOR THE SHOULDER BLOCK

These blocks are any blocks in which contact with the defender can be made on the first step. The technique to be taught is to drive off, or uncoil from stance, stepping with the foot on the side (or shoulder) you will hit with. Drive the head between the defender and the point of attack. Bring up the flipper for extension and power. Aim at defender's middle (hit them where they bend). After contact, drive up (look for the sky) and follow through.

### One-on-one

Use the same drill as when drilling for the fireout block, only change the technique. By driving the head to one side or the other, the block changes from driving the defender back to turning him in one direction or the other.

### Crowther sled drill by the numbers

This drill reduces the action to one step. Have the center make his pass to the QB and make his forward move with his back foot. He should be aligned close enough to the blocking pad of the sled to make contact on his first step. By holding the action at this point, the center can be corrected on position. He should come up strong with the shoulder and flipper as he makes that one step. His position is now uncoiled from his stance, but his front foot is still anchored. His back is straight and his shoulders are square. His line of force is from the lead foot (now on the ground) through his legs, back and shoulder on a power line through the blocking pad, through the supports into the heart of the sled. If you stand behind the center, this power line is very evident. The blocker should do this first step, daily, a number of times. Of course, the drill is by the numbers, so the second step is with the foot that is now back. He should gain ground on this step. His off arm and hand (the side not in contact with the sled) can do one of two things. First, he may put it to the ground for support and balance, or he may continue to pump this arm in a running fashion. Step three is the follow-through.

### One-step drill on the big sled

Use a seven-man sled and put seven balls on the ground in front of each blocking pad. The center starts at one end or the other and makes the exchange to the QB and executes a one-step "pop" into the pad. He quickly aligns in front the next pad and does the same thing and so on until he has gone down the line.

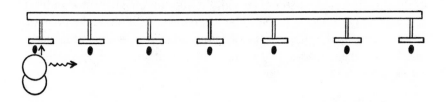

DIAGRAM #9

### Bag drill

Utilize a standing dummy. On this drill you may start out with the "by the numbers drill." Here again you work on the first step and pop, the second step, and finally the follow-through.

### Bag drill on the plank

Because shoulder blocks usually end up in turning the defender, you want a much shorter plank. It should be just long enough to establish a good base. Three feet long placed at the point of the ball is plenty. You can utilize the long plank by starting the drill at the end of the plank.

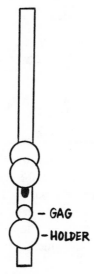

— GAG

—HOLDER

**DIAGRAM #10**

### Hand shield and apron drill

The center should use the same techniques but by using either hand shields or blocking aprons on the defensive man, you will get more realistic reaction than from the standing dummy. Also you must keep stressing "block up" or "stay up." The worst habit offensive line blockers can get into is to go to the ground, or block down.

### Nose drill

This is a one-on-one situation. The coach should stand behind the defensive man. The defensive man is aligned directly on the ball. The coach gives hand signals to the center indicating a right-shoulder or left-shoulder block. (This same drill can incorporate fireout blocks, reverse blocks, etc.) The center makes the exchange on cadence and executes the block indicated by the hand signal. The defensive man reacts by "reading" the block, since there is no flow of the ball; however, the center coach should always have someone on the center's nose during skeleton back drills or any other offensive drill incorporating the centers. In other words, never let your center just pass the ball to the quarterback without someone, alive or dummy, on his nose.

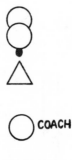

DIAGRAM #11

### Running shoulder blocks drill

The same techniques are used but the center must run some distance to get to the defender. At the point of contact, all the same fundamentals apply. Place two flat hand shields two paces from the center and put a linebacker between the two markers. The center makes the exchange and drives to the defender and blocks him exactly the same only with a running start.

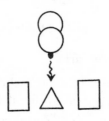

DIAGRAM #12

### Pull and shoulder blocks drill

In many offensive schemes, the center is called upon to pull and block defensive ends or blitzing outside linebackers. These are usually bootleg or reverse pass plays or some form of pass protection; however, since the run option exists, the center must master these techniques. Set up a defender to the center's outside. Place towels where contact is most likely. Have the center make the exchange and don't forget he must still move forward with his back foot first or else the timing of the exchange will be jeopardized. The center then pulls back to the contact area and executes a shoulder block on the oncoming defender.

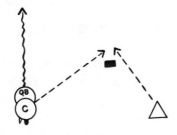

DIAGRAM #13

## 6. DRILLING FOR THE REACH BLOCK

These blocks are the most difficult blocks any offensive lineman must make. They are blocks against leverage. Some coaches call this "blocking uphill." The idea is to tie up or contain a defender who is already outside the blocker and keep him from penetration or lateral pursuit. This is never used as a key block at the point of attack. Reach blocks are usually used on wide plays only. The blocker must use quickness and scramble to stay up on the block. The aiming point is the outside leg. The blocker must open with his outside leg first in a lateral move. He must get his head and shoulders under the defender's hands and strive for a "bite" on the defender's outside leg. From there on it is a contest of determination to keep this outside contact as the defender tries to shuffle out. Again, the worst mistake is to go to the ground. Pressure on the defender is the only way this block can be successful. In drilling for this block, you must use a live situation with people who will react laterally. Place the defender outside the center, either on or off the line of scrimmage. After the exchange, the center executes these techniques.

DIAGRAM #14

## 7. DRILLS FOR THE REVERSE BLOCK

There are two kinds of reverse blocks: one, the blocker executes a fireout block on a defender directly over him and, after stopping the defender's charge, goes into a quick reverse to "pin" the defender; the other type of reverse is when the defender is one man removed from the blocker, and the blocker must simply fill a gap or hole away from the flow of the ball. This is opposite from the reach block because the blocker is blocking away from the point of attack.

First, drill for the reverse block when the defender is head on. Use the one-on-one setup as previously described. Use any or all the training aids available, such as bags, aprons, shields, or defensive players. After exchange, the center blocks as if he were executing a fireout block. When he has at least earned a tie with the defender, he drives his outside arm (if the point of attack is to his right side, he uses his right arm, if the point of attack is to his left side, he uses his left arm) across in front of the defender. This creates a reverse or whipping action with the rest of his body. His outside leg will come up to the outside in a natural manner. The blocker is now pinned and his forward momentum should only make pursuit that much more difficult.

**DIAGRAM #15**

Drill for reverse blocks when the defender is down or away from the blocker. These blocks are sometimes called "check-back blocks." Set up the defender in the proper spacing. Have the center make the exchange. He should always make a lead step (step off with the foot closest to the defender). This will assure contact with the off shoulder and off foot at the same time. The center aims his head in front of the defender's charge. This position is most important because penetration must be shut off first. If the defender is playing a waiting game, and doesn't charge, then the blocker has achieved his first goal, but can only use the reverse action to impede the defender's pursuit angle. A quick blocker can do both—shut off penetration and force a bad pursuit angle. His lead on the defender is most important. If he leads him too much he will not get enough "bite" to prevent pursuit. If he doesn't lead him enough, the defender can get penetration. Generally speaking, however, this is not a difficult block. All the angle of force is with the blocker. If he gets his head in the right place to start with, the defender will usually take himself out of the play. This block should be used to fill holes left by pulling guards or whenever the defense is using a gap defense on short yardage situations. It should not be used against floating or reading defenders. It makes this drill more realistic if a pulling guard is aligned next to the center. Place the defender in the gap and declare a short-yardage or goal-line situation.

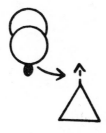

DIAGRAM #16

## 8. DRILLING FOR OPEN-FIELD BLOCKING

Centers should be accomplished open-field blockers because they are often uncovered on the line of scrimmage. In general, their open-field blocks fall into two categories: one, the center must block a middle linebacker who has beat him on the snap and is heading for the point of attack (either through great reaction or predetermined stunting); the other is commonly called a downfield block. This is where the gravy is. This kind of blocking makes touchdowns out of normal running plays.

### Close open-field blocking drill

Set up a middle linebacker against your center. Place hand shields near where the inside of the off-tackle hole should be. Use a running back to give flow of the ball. Tell the defender which way the ball will flow; this will give him the edge and almost make it impossible for the center to cut him off in the middle. The center makes the exchange and the QB takes and hands to the running back. The running back must run outside the hand shields. The center must stay up and after the linebacker knowing sooner or later the linebacker must come to collection to make the tackle. When this happens, the center drives his head between the defender and his running back and drives him out. The running back cuts back on this block.

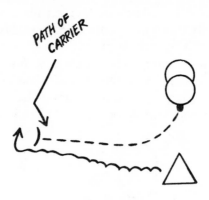

DIAGRAM #17

### Downfield roll blocking drill

The open-field blocking drill should most always be done against standing dummies, except in live breakdown or scrimmage drills. The reason here is that individual downfield blocking drills are done with a good long running start, and will produce a lot of injuries if done live. The technique can be mastered against bags. Keep in mind that perfect position by the blocker is effective even if the block is incorrect. Just the fact that a body is in the pursuit path is enough to spring a good runner. What you must teach is morale and technique so that maximum punishment is inflicted on the defender and not the blocker. You must eliminate the cause of missed downfield blocks, which is usually leaving the feet too soon. A good way to teach when to "throw" the block is when the blocker is within handshaking distance. Because defenders will give with the "throw" it is advisable to teach three body rolls after contact with the bag. The technique to be taught is for the running blocker to drive into the bag (or man) using a rolling action. Contact is made with the back of the shoulder and a continuous rolling action takes place. The blockers should keep their elbows in close to their bodies to prevent injury.

### Roll blocking drill vs. secondary setup

Set up four standing dummies, without holders, in positions of a four-deep secondary facing the center. The center makes the exchange and fires down field for dummy number one. He makes a shoulder-roll block, rolling three times. He sets the bag back up for the next center. When all centers have blocked dummy number one, they go to number two and so on until all have been blocked.

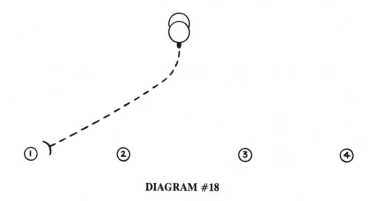

DIAGRAM #18

### Downfield blocking drill for reaction

Set the standing dummies in a triangle formation. After the exchange, the center drives toward the middle of the formation. When he arrives at the "crossroads," the coach hollers out which dummy to block.

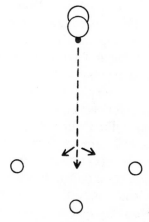

DIAGRAM #19

### Downfield blocking drill for position

This is done live, but only position is stressed. Set up a corner-back or safetyman. On the snap, the defensive man reacts up. The center takes the angle to cut him off. At the point of contact, the center merely uses a two-hand tag to simulate the block. This gives realistic reaction to the blocker but eliminates contact, thereby reducing the possibility of injury.

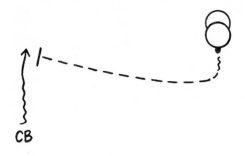

DIAGRAM #20

## 9. PASS BLOCK, RUN ACTION DRILLS

Run action passes feature fakes into the line or pullups and sprint-outs. There is no need to differentiate between regular blocking and pass blocking when faking a run into the line. Every lineman should block the run even if it turns into a pass. However, pullups, sprintouts and bootlegs have one thing in common that is different from line blocking, that is, the throwing area is outside, or moving to the out-side. It is most important that all interior linemen know what area they are protecting. One good expression that will help you teach this is, "Always keep the end of your spine pointing at the passer." Here is a position drill for blocking for run action passes.

Set up the center and QB on a line of scrimmage. Call the various pass plays that have the QB throwing from different places. After the exchange, the QB executes his fakes, or sprints, and then sets up to throw. The center positions himself to block. At this point, blow the whistle and see if you can "site" down the middle of the blocker's back straight to the passer. By quickly going through all the different types of QB actions your centers will learn, by habit, the proper blocking position. By adding a live or dummy rusher to this position drill, you can work on the individual pass blocking.

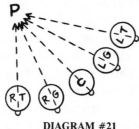

DIAGRAM #21

## 10. PASS BLOCKING, DROP-BACK ACTION DRILLS

Again, position is the most important fundamental. The blocker must be positioned so that the rusher must go "through" him. Again "ass to the passer" may sound crude, but there is no other way to express this position.

### Drop drill

The center makes the exchange (always makes jab step with back foot first even though he is going to drop back) and then bounces back about one yard. This is not a hard and fast rule, but the distance of his drop must never bring him closer than six yards from the passer. Assuming the passer sets up at seven yards, his drop should be one yard. Many coaches will tell you that a four- or five-yard distance from "wall" to passer is inviting batted passes from the rushers—even though they have not broken through the blocking "cup." Any time you see a drop-back passer setting up at five yards, you know you can cause him a lot of trouble by just getting your hands up. There is one exception: if the passer is quite tall and has a high release, the wall or cup can be closer to him without creating problems. Also, don't confuse this rule with the "quick series" passes. On these, the QB only drops two yards. This means the line blockers must fire out on this type of action.

After the center's one-yard drop, check him for quickness and position. He must flex at the knees, keep his back straight and bounce on the balls of his feet. All the driving action of a pass block must come from the legs. If the back is humped, the legs will be straight and then force will be "up from the trunk" instead of "forward from the legs."

### Pop drill

This is a one-on-one blocking drill which teaches the blocker to stop the rusher's charge. After exchange and drop, the center has good knee flex and straight back and times the leg extension. This is an uncoiling action. The back must remain straight; the hitting point is the top of the forehead; the aiming point on the rusher is the numbers on his jersey; the hands are against the chest. This is a short "explosion." The head gear only travels about six inches, so the extension must be timed properly. Considering the speed of the rusher, the blow must be struck when the rusher and blocker are only about a foot apart. A small man can stop a big man with this technique. There is no foot action in this drill. Both feet remain in place. After the center "pops" the rusher and learns the technique, go on to the next phase. Use one-on-one setup.

### Pop and recoil drill

After the "pop" both rusher and blocker will recoil to varying degrees. The blocker must determine what the rusher does next. If the rusher comes on again hard, the blocker can "pop" again and again, always staying with his "ass to the passer," or he can go into a "cut" block. The cut block is particularly good because it chops the rusher down and provides for good passer vision and throwing lanes. (This is considering a five-second or less pass protection time.) Use one-on-one setup with the center. Have him exchange, set and pop. Make him judge as to the proper course to take: either continue to pop and recoil or use a cut block.

### Facing drill

Use the same setup; however, there is no contact in this drill. When rusher gets to arm length from blocker, he tries to make lateral head nods or feints to maneuver the blocker out of position. Coaching point: the blocker should never "pop" a dancer; he should simply shuffle his feet to stay square.

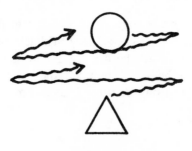

**DIAGRAM #22**

### Full pass-blocking drill

Using one-on-one setup, give the rusher the choice as to whether he will lay his ears back and come hard or dance around. This creates the decision situation. These are individual drills. Blocking patterns come up under group and semi-group drills.

### Heavy bag drill

By using a heavy bag suspended from a metal frame so that it will swing, much can be done to teach proper pop and recoil methods of pass blocking.

## 11. CENTER SNAP DRILLS

### Loosening-up drill

Centers should always stretch their groin and upper-leg muscles. Centers take as wide a stance as possible and then try to touch the ground with their elbows. Next they should push against their knees from the inside with their elbows. They should also use the toe tapper with their legs crossed. Another good one is sometimes called the "mountain climber." From a standing position, they step out as far as they can and lean out over the extended leg so that the chest touches the knee. At the same time, grasp both arms under the extended leg. Still another is called "chase the bunny." From the forward leaning rest position, the centers alternate swinging their feet forward. When really loose, they can easily get their feet (alternately) out in front of their hands.

### Grip and wrist-snap drill

Centers can do this together. Two centers pair off and throw two-handed overhead passes to each other. They should use the same grip they will use when in a centering position. There is some degree of variance in grips used by different centers. Size of the individual's hands is a major factor. The smaller the hand, the farther back on the ball is a general rule. Most centers like the laces under the tips of the fingers on the passing hand, if possible. The other hand is usually on top of the ball or slightly off center, away from the passing hand. The thumbs almost touch. The top hand helps produce the spiral. At the end of the arm action, the wrists snap and the hands give the ball a clockwise spin. In working with youngsters, you will find they need to almost get the passing hand under the ball in order to get a good spiral. This drill from the upright position should help them develop the right passing technique.

### Heavy-ball drill

These weighted balls are invaluable for training for the long snap. Always start from the down, or centering, position. Check the width of the stance. It must be wider than the T-formation center stance; however, it can be too wide: it is too wide when the center must collect himself back together in order to block or release downfield. Have the centers snap to one another from only a distance of five yards using the weighted ball. Gradually the distance can be increased up to ten yards. Do not use weighted balls for longer snaps. Always have the centers point with their index finger after releasing the ball. They should, of course, point at the target. This will insure a good follow-through.

### 14-yard snap drill

Use a regulation ball and always provide a target. After the preliminary short-distance snapping drills, go to the 14-yard snap. Here the key word is "speed." This snap must have speed of arm and wrist action and speed on the flight of the ball. Always stress this to your centers. At first, they will tend to try for the pretty spiral. Usually this results in a rainbow-type trajectory because of the care the center is placing on spiral rather than speed. You must make him sacrifice spiral at first in favor of speed. If necessary, cut back on the distance but gradually work back to 14 yards. It takes a lot of work to get the speed snap with the good spiral. Again, don't accept spiral over speed. When the center really tries to "burn" one back he will often lift the ball from the ground first. This gives him leverage from which he can put maximum power and wrist snap. This can be overdone, but if the action is quick there is nothing wrong with lifting the ball first. "Dragging" the ball is preferred because you are less apt to get the nose of the ball out of the proper plane. If, by lifting the ball, you can achieve greater speed on the ball, then that's what should be done. Speed is the answer.

### Snap accuracy drill

Very often your center may want to practice his snaps when there is no one around to catch him up. This before and after practice time can be invaluable in developing individual skills. Have the center take a bag of balls and hit the field by himself. Have available a training aid for a target. Canvas stretched between goal-post uprights, with suitable markings is one aid that is helpful. Another idea is a wooden frame nailed on to the top of a low hurdle. There should be a space wide enough for the ball to pass through. The middle of this space is equal to the height of a point on the human leg halfway between the knee and the hip. Set this target up at 13 yards.

### Snap to holder drill

Use a center, a holder and a ball boy. Center snaps to holder at the exact distance (7 yards) used for field goals and extra-point attempts. Holder should go through his routine of receiving and placing the ball for the kick. He then passes the ball back to the ball boy who hands the ball back to the center. The distance should be easy for the center after working on the long snap. In this technique the center should not have to lift the ball in order to get a straight line shot to the holder. Dragging the ball should keep the nose down and give the proper trajectory; therefore, it is much preferred. Practice will develop consistency, and consistency is what you must strive for with your kicking tandem. There is a definite rhythm between the center, holder and kicker. If the center delivers the ball to the holder at a different place every time, the rhythm will be destroyed. The only way to develop consistency is practice.

## 12. DRILL FOR PUNT PROTECTION BLOCKING

To be perfectly honest about it, you can't expect much of a blocking job from your center and still get a great snap. Let's look at the priority of things. First the snap—then the center must get his head up quickly. Next the center tries to get a square lick on any opponent over him or in either gap. Lastly, he releases downfield to get into tackling position. Any block the center makes in protecting the kicker is a bonus. He does fill up a space and one of the reasons you work on this is so the center can protect himself. It has become fun and games to put a rough guy on the center's nose and run through him, even though such actions will never block a kick. The idea is to intimidate the center into making a bad snap on the next punt formation. By work, the center can make the snap, get his head up and be in a position to absorb the blow without getting rolled back like a rug. The main thing a center can do is take the edge off a punt rusher in his area without slowing down his own release downfield.

## 13. DRILL FOR FIELD GOAL AND
## EXTRA-POINT BLOCKING

The center is a vital part of the blocking pattern in these situations. His snap is much easier and he can snap to a blocking position quicker. He is the pivotal point in the protection area. After the snap, the center should come to a hitting position—sometimes called the basketball guarding position. He uses a small backwards hop and uses his elbows and shoulders to make contact with rushers. He never moves his feet but can still often block both gaps by his shoulder action. These are containing blocks and, if he gives some ground, no harm is done. The main thing is to prevent a crack in the wall. In drilling for this block, you set up two dummies, one touching each foot (after stance) to simulate the offensive guards. Place one or two rushers in various in-line or linebacker positions who rush on the snap. They must come between the dummies. The center stays square to the line of scrimmage and fills the hole.

## 14. DRILLS FOR TACKLING

All offensive linemen in college and high school must cover punts and all offensive personnel must switch to defense on a quick turnover; therefore, they should have a limited time for drilling on the fundamentals of tackling. Since you are limited in time, the coach should only drill on two basics.

### Pursuit drill

Most offensive linemen need to be aware of angles of pursuit. The main thing to teach in this drill is to take an angle that will intercept the path of the ball carrier, and then square up. At this point, a two-hand tag is enough since you are emphasizing position. Put the center on the ground, on his back in a prone position. Have a ballcarrier ten yards from the center facing him. At the command "ball" the center scrambles to his feet and the back with the ball breaks towards either sideline. The center stalks him running laterally and giving ground. The center must keep his shoulder square with the ballcarrier so he can handle cutbacks. He must maintain an interception angle laterally. When in position to tackle, he uses a two-handed tag.

### Open-field tackling drill

Mark an area with lines three yards apart, eight yards long. Give the ballcarrier a ball and place him in the middle of one of the horizontal lines facing the center. Each has his restraining line. The ballcarrier has eight yards laterally to maneuver. The center's job is to tackle the ballcarrier before he reaches his restraining line. On the command "ball," the ballcarrier can make any moves he wants, but tries to reach the other line. The center is now free to tackle the ballcarrier any way he wants to with the idea being to defend his line. This drill allows for full-speed tackling in an open field, but reduces the injury element because of the three-yard distance.

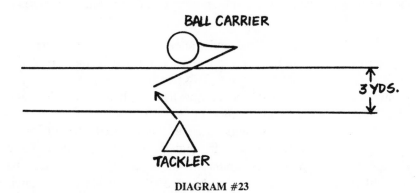

DIAGRAM #23

## B. GUARDS AND TACKLES

### 1. DRILL FOR THE STANCE

*Circle drill*

All guards and tackles form a large circle with the coach in the middle. They all face the coach for explanation and demonstration. It is a good idea to teach this "by the numbers."

*"One"*—Everyone places his feet slightly wider than his shoulders and staggers back his right foot, so that the end of the toe of the staggered foot is even with the instep of the "up" foot.

*"Two"*—Everyone flexes his knees and places his elbows on the top of his knees.

*"Three"*—Reach out with the right arm (if left foot is staggered, reach out with left arm) and lean forward until right hand hits the ground. The weight should now be equally distributed on three points: the down hand, the toe of the staggered foot, and the ball of the up foot. The down hand may be supported either by a knuckle spread or a finger spread. Usually short-armed players will prefer the finger spread as it keeps the shoulder line a bit higher.

*"Four"*—Take the up arm off the knee and allow it to hang in *front* of the up-knee. This creates almost a four-point stance, but not quite. It is an optional maneuver. Many great players rest the up-arm on the up-knee and block like demons. The only advantage in the arm hanging in front of the knee is that it keeps the shoulder line parallel to the line of scrimmage. When the up-arm rests on the knee, it causes a slight tilt in the shoulder line.

*"Five"*—Raise the head and flatten the back. A good way to explain this action is to imagine a drawstring tied to the top of the headgear and the end of the spine. This imaginary string keeps getting tighter and tighter. A good blocker must have his head up and his back so flat that he would make a good table.

Other coaching points about stance: the stance described above has a good deal of weight forward and is excellent for the running game; however, when a lineman has to pull or pass block, he should be settled back more over his legs without so much weight on his down hand. (This is another reason for hanging the off-arm as it disguises the forward pitch of the stance.)

## 2. DRILL FOR STARTS

The offensive line of scrimmage must move as one unit. Ragged starts produce poor timing. This aspect of offensive drilling is pretty dull and requires some imagination to keep it interesting. Later on in this book the group aspect will cover many ways to drill for line starts as a unit. The individual can only drill on his ability to "come out of the blocks" and keep his body low on the first few steps.

### Individual starting drill

Use a shoot or any other training aid that will make the lineman fire out at the proper height. Even a simple rope stretched across poles will do the trick. Also, use the ten-foot plank. Have the lineman assume the proper stance and give him the team cadence. He times his explosion off the line to the starting signal and drives forward ten yards. He should be checked on his arm action and running form. However, concerning the height of the training aid used to control the height of the lineman's charge, it should never be so low that he must "waddle" to get under it. The only thing you are trying to prevent is immediate raising up from the stance. Experimentation will give you the proper distance from the ground the barrier should be.

There is another training aid that is good for young players. It is called a cage, and is simply a wooden frame approximately ten yards square with eight leg supports at five-yard intervals. The whole area should be covered with chicken wire. The lowest part is approximately 56″ from the ground. Linemen can not only practice starts under this cage but also work on their pull techniques. Further, by using dummies just outside the cage, you can work on all types of running blocks.

## 3. INDIVIDUAL BLOCKING DRILLS

All of the basic blocks and the drills to teach them are covered under "Center Individual Drills." They are the fireout block, the shoulder block, the reach block, the reverse block, the open-field block, all the pass blocks and the tackling drills. Guards and tackles should do all the above individual drills just as given for the centers. There are a few drills that are different, and these are as follows:

## 4. DRILLS FOR PULLING

### Basic Teaching Drill

Make a large circle with all the guards and tackles. Have all people assume the same foot position as in their football stance. They should flex at the knees and place both elbows on their sides with the arms bent in a fighter's position. The first move to drill on is a simultaneous pivoting on the left toe and placing the right foot out at a 45° angle.

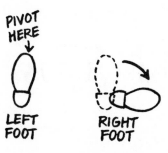

PIVOT HERE

LEFT FOOT        RIGHT FOOT

DIAGRAM #24

Notice that the right foot gains very little ground laterally. You simply pick it up and point it to the side. After the linemen do this move several times, they should be able to do it smoothly. The next move is to combine the pull of the right arm. Stress this heavily. The arm pull should be so strong that it actually pulls the whole trunk and right leg around. Putting the pivot on the left foot, the changing direction of the right foot, along with the whipping action of the right arm should be done quite a few times until all have the move down pat. The next step is to have the linemen go to the three-point stance and repeat the same action. Add the following coaching points. The right arm, at the end of the whipping action, should show well above the back; the left arm should go to the ground to keep from falling down. This is still just a one-step move. Let's review. On the hike, pivot on the left toe, step from straight to right with the right foot, whip the right arm hard until it shows over the back, catch yourself with the left arm bracing on the ground. Hold this position for the coaching check. Continue to stress the action of the whipping right arm while the linemen do this one move over and over. The last step in the drill is simply to sprint from this position. Of course, the left arm won't have to go down now because of the continuous action. When the linemen can do this reasonably well, have them form single-file lines and come up to a center with a ball (so a line of scrimmage can be established) two at a time. On cadence, they execute a pull to the right together. It is a good idea to have a standing dummy in the offensive tackle position so they will have to "pull out" rather than cross over. All this should be repeated, from the beginning, when going to the left. You will notice that pulling to the left is difficult since the left foot is usually the "up" foot. Actually, I've experimented with linemen changing their stance when going to the left, that is, staggering the left foot back instead of the right. It was never noticed by the defense, and it makes the pulling move a lot easier.

DIAGRAM #25

### Drilling for the short trap

The shortest trap is a gap-cross block. The next shortest is trapping an even-line defense. Longer traps are trapping a 5-4 tackle, 60 tackle, 5-4 end and, lastly, a 60 end. The trapper must be ready to "trap on course." In other words, he runs a specific route and as soon as he clears his checkback or power block, he blocks inside out on the first opposite color that crosses his path. It is most important that the trapper drill on his footwork for all these traps. When he moves his "onside" foot, it must point in the direction of his route. Diagram #26 should show the proper placement of the onside foot for the different traps. The longer they get the greater the angle from straight ahead. Tackles should drill on all these traps also.

DIAGRAM #26

I want to follow Diagram #26 with another (Diagram #27), showing the route to take to always insure an inside-out approach to the defender.

DIAGRAM #27

Set up standing bags with holders in the different positions and have the trapper execute his short traps.

### Drilling for the long pull

This always entails getting the on-foot deeper than parallel on the first step. It also entails getting turned upfield after paralleling the line of scrimmage. The onside, or lead guard (assuming that both guards are pulling), should always turn a sharp curve and look to the inside; the following (or off-guard) should turn upfield wider or block to the outside. Neither should think about heading for the goal line unless everyone on defense has fallen down. This diagram will show the guards' routes. Have them block standing dummies.

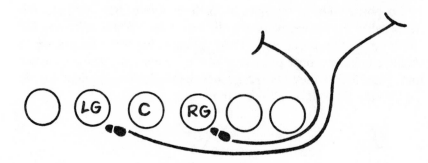

**DIAGRAM #28**

### Drilling for the short curve

Different positions on the offense will be required to run tight curves and maintain balance, but guards and tackles do it more often. This action takes place after cross-blocking or pulling. Use any marker to designate the hole and place a standing dummy in an appropriate position. The guard or tackle takes his stance and runs the route (which includes a tight turn). A logical place for this drill is the goal-post. The linemen take a stance in the middle of the two uprights with the down-hand on the end zone line. On cadence, they pull to the right or left and turn as soon as they clear the upright. By placing a standing dummy and holder inside, the linemen are forced to run a very tight curve. Coaching points are: dropping the inside shoulder; good arm action; looking back to the inside; short steps; good base; support by the inside hand on the ground if slipping occurs.

**DIAGRAM #29**

### Drilling for the trap with a two-man sled

Place the trapper the proper distance and direction from the sled.

On cadence, he pulls and executes an inside-out shoulder block on the upright of the Crowther sled. If he doesn't hit low and drive up, the spring in the blocking upright will throw him back.

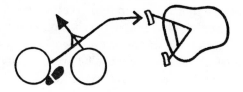

DIAGRAM #30

### Drilling for the trap using the cage

One of the big errors in technique when trapping is for the trapper to raise up on the pull. When he gets to where he is going, he has to get down again in order to make the block. To cure this, put him under the cage and place a dummy and holder just outside in the proper angle from the trapper. This will make him stay low on the pull and throughout the approach. He is now in position to hit low and block up.

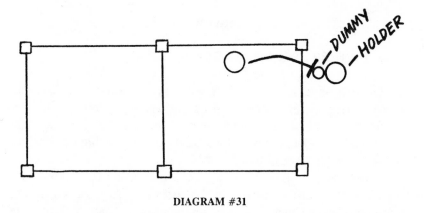

DIAGRAM #31

### Drilling for the log in

The most difficult defensive man to trap is the player who is aligned as the logical man to be trapped, but who, after snap of the ball, makes an inside or pinching charge. If the trapper makes a perfect approach, the two meet almost head on. Since it is now almost impossible for the trapper to move this man out of the hole, he must take him beyond the point of attack. To do this he must use a technique called "logging." This calls for a change in direction, so a reverse action is called for. The trapper butts at the defender with his head and shoulders and immediately goes into a reverse or turning action. This means just going with the force of the defender. If the defender is not pinching hard, but merely shuffling laterally into the hole, the trapper must make a decision to either blast him out of the hole or log him in. This is most difficult to teach against bags or training aids. It should be drilled in a one-on-one situation. The form can be practiced at half speed, but the real thing is the only answer. Set up markers for other players and spacing. Have the defender wait, charge, shuffle in, or pinch in hard and make the trapper block accordingly. Since this type of skeleton drill gives the defender the advantage, it is good to use defensive players of lesser ability.

DIAGRAM #32

## 5. PUNT PROTECTION BLOCKING DRILL

Guards and tackles use a different punt protection technique than do the centers; therefore, they must be drilled separately. Techniques vary as to the type of punt formation used, but the most popular is the spread, or 9-man front, formation. Here are the coaching points and drill setup for the spread punt:

Guards align two to three feet from their center (depending on a normal or "loaded" situation in the middle). They use an upright stance with either hands or elbows on their knees. They look over the defensive alignment. If it is more than man-for-man inside they call "loaded"; if it is man-for-man or less, they make no call. On loaded situations, they hop back one step on the snap. Their rule is inside, over, outside. This means that if there is a defender between them and their center, they must block "inside." If there is no man between them and their center, they block head on; no man head on, they block first man to their outside. The block used is similar to the "pop" in pass blocking. The main coaching point is for them to get square on the rusher and not strike a glancing or side blow. After stopping the rusher's first charge, the blocker recoils and releases in predetermined lanes (covered under team kicking drills). They must not get tied up after the initial pop. Place the guards in proper position and vary the position of one rusher. On cadence the rusher uses various types of charges and the blocker attempts a "square bite" on the rusher and then releases.

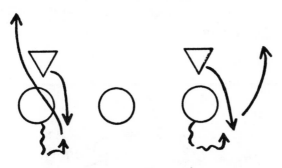

DIAGRAM #33

The tackles always align at three feet from their guards. Another way to express this is to take a split that is the distance of one man's stance. The blocking techniques are exactly the same as the guards', except they never hop backwards when the defense is loaded. They might have to hop sideways (inside or outside) to meet their blocking requirements, but never backwards. Also, the tackles know their first responsibility is inside when their guard calls "loaded." Use the same setup as the one used for the guards.

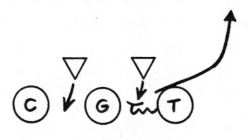

DIAGRAM #34

## 6. EXTRA-POINT AND FIELD-GOAL PROTECTION DRILL

These drills are rarely done individually, but it is a good idea for a coach to work with one player during specialty period, or after practice, on these skills. The coaching point involved in this kind of blocking is for the blocker to anchor his outside foot and never move it. By body sway and shoulder and flipper lunge, the blocker can seal both gaps if necessary. He does not want to get much weight forward because he can be pulled or turned leaving a gap.

Put the blocker between two standing dummies in a hitting position. Use one or two rushers to come through his position. Make the blocker get a solid shoulder, or shoulders, on one or two rushers. Stress keeping the anchor foot in place.

DIAGRAM #35

## C. TIGHT ENDS

### 1. DRILL FOR THE STANCE

Place the tight ends in a circle or abreast of each other and have them go through the following steps to a good stance:

*One*—Feet apart only slightly wider than the shoulders.

*Two*—Elbows on knees.

*Three*—Stagger back right foot (left, if lefthanded) until toe of right foot is even with heel of left foot. Since many tight ends are the tallest linemen, you may find they need a more pronounced stagger The longer the legs, the more the stagger.

*Four*—Reach out with the arm on the side of the stagger and go to the ground, making a three-point stance. Tight ends must be able to release on a pass route so they do not have nearly as much weight forward on the down-arm. Also, it is not quite as important that they hang the off-arm in front of the up-knee. Balance and the ability to make lateral releases must dominate the tight end stance.

*Five*—Straighten the back and lift the head. Tight ends are also key blockers.

## 2. DRILLS FOR STARTS

Tight ends use the same starting drills as outlined for other offensive line positions.

## 3. DRILLS FOR FIREOUT BLOCKS, SHOULDER BLOCKS, REACH BLOCKS, REVERSE BLOCKS, OPEN-FIELD BLOCKS, PASS BLOCKS, PUNT BLOCKS, EXTRA-POINT AND FIELD-GOAL PROTECTION BLOCKS AND TACKLING

These drills and techniques are described for other offensive linemen and should be applied to the tight ends also. However, there are some drills and techniques that are peculiar to tight ends and they are as follows:

## 4. RELEASE DRILLS

*One-on-one releases:* Place one defender on the nose of the tight end with only one assignment. Try to prevent a release. The tight ends must now go full-speed against this defender.

*Techniques:*

> Inside or outside low drive
> Single fake and break opposite
> Wide pull (if route allows)

*Two-on-one releases:* Place two defenders on the nose of the tight end with only one purpose—to hold the tight end from making a release.

*Techniques:*

> Straight ahead submarine release on all fours
> Inside or outside pivot
> Wide pull

## 5. ROUTE DRILLS

Tight ends will have a certain set number of pass routes. They are predetermined and require much practice to be exact. Place markers, such as towels, at key places in the route. Breaks or turns should be marked. For beginners, a chalk line is a good way to start out. These routes should be run both with a defender in the way and without interference. Another dimension to these route-running drills is to have a dropping linebacker provide harrassment. Tight ends in particular must learn to run routes and arrive at the reception point at the proper time, despite the fact that they receive more obstacles than do wide receivers. Further, it must be made clear that route running, like faking, is *good* if it draws a crowd. This means someone else is open.

## 6. CATCH DRILLS

### Pitch and catch drill

Station two tight ends about five yards apart. Use as many units of two as possible. Give each unit a football. They play catch but throw high and low, right and left. Gradually increase the distance apart to 10 or 15 yards.

**DIAGRAM #36**

## 7. REACTION DRILL

Line up all the tight ends in single file. Have a passer (or coach) stand behind them, just to the right or left with a football ready to pass. Use the starting cadence. The end in front of the line takes off straight downfield. On his second step, he looks for the ball. The passer purposely throws the ball to various positions around the receiver that are difficult to catch, but not impossible. The receiver must adjust quickly. Make sure the receiver will fight to come back for a ball that is thrown short.

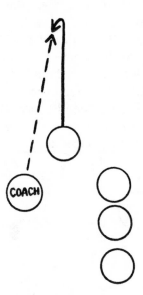

DIAGRAM #37

## 8. LOOK THE BALL INTO THE HANDS DRILL

Line up the tight ends in single file and, one at a time, have them run pass routes. The quarterback takes from the center, sets up on rhythm and throws to the receiver. The key point in the drill is to use special balls. There should be a total of four or five balls, each with a two-inch number painted on each quadrant of the ball. Balls should be #2, #3, #4 and #5. Eliminate #1 as it is too easy to see. The receiver calls the number of the ball as he catches it. This will force him to "look the ball" into his hands.

DIAGRAM #38

## 9. MACHINE GUN DRILL

Place four ends in a half-moon formation; give one a football. They face a lone end about seven yards away. The lone end also has a football. On the command "Go," the lone end throws his ball to one of the four facing him. At the same time, the end in the half-moon formation fires his ball at the lone end out in front. A rapid exchange takes place. The lone man out front must receive without fumbling and must pass while the second ball is on its way. The instant he fumbles, he is "out" and his place is taken by one of the men in the formation. Score can be kept to provide competition.

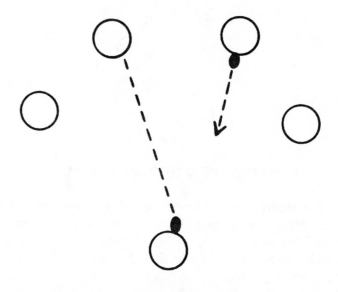

DIAGRAM #39

## 10. SIDELINE DRILL

Set up a center and quarterback six yards from the hash mark into the middle of the field. Place the ends on the hash and one at a time they run a sideline cut. Have either a dummy or live defensive back facing the ends. The ends run a 8-9 yard sideline route and receive the ball just before going out of bounds.

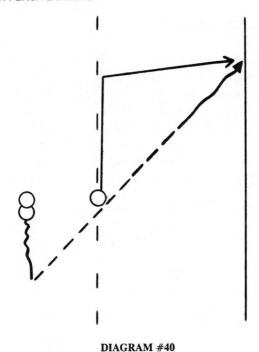

**DIAGRAM #40**

## 11. FIGHT FOR THE BALL

Form three ends in a loose triangle facing a passer at a distance of ten yards. The passer throws into the formation and the receivers contest each other for the ball. The passer should vary his aim so the ball cannot be anticipated.

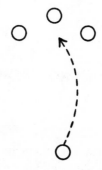

**DIAGRAM #41**

### 12. QUICK CATCH DRILL

Station a tight end about 8 to 10 yards from a passer with his back turned to the passer. The passer hollers "Go" and throws a pass at the same time. The receiver hops around quickly on the command "Go" and is forced to receive the pass without seeing it leave the passer's hand. The passer should vary the passes—right and left side and high and low. This is a good drill to develop hand and eye coordination. Also, it is a good time to emphasize the "thumbs rule." When facing the passer, if the pass is below the waist, the thumbs are out, if the pass is above the waist, the thumbs are in.

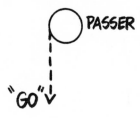

DIAGRAM #42

## D. DRILLS FOR RUNNING BACKS

### 1. STANCE DRILL

Every day the offensive running backs should spend a few minutes on stance. This should continue on through the season. Also, if shifting is involved, this too should be incorporated into the stance drill. It is absolutely essential that the offensive backs start with perfect balance. Their starts range from straight ahead to lateral. Since they are much more noticeable than the linemen, they must achieve the same stance on every play. If care is not taken, a back will lean forward on straight ahead shots and settle back when going laterally. These small tendencies can be picked up by the defense and reduce the one important edge offense has—surprise.

There are many variations of backfield stances and they fluctuate according to the offensive cycle of any particular time. Right now the offensive trends are run-oriented. This means most teams will feature their backs "down," or with a three-, even four-point stance. The classic T-formation, in its beginnings, called for an upright or two-point stance. This old offense was a thing of beauty, and it would not be surprising to see it return in some form or another. The philosophy was opposite those of the split-T, the veer, the I, and the Wishbone, which are being used today. All these formations are tinged with single-wing philosophy. The old T featured much more faking, counters, reverses and lateral moves. In teaching these two basic stances (up and down), it will be easier to start with the "down" stance. It is easier because it has already been described under the section dealing with offensive linemen. The stance is basically the same, but there are a couple of different coaching points. Offensive backs should not have quite so much weight forward and they should not have quite so much stagger. Otherwise, it is the same stance. The "up" stance is taught by starting with the feet. The base should not be wider than the shoulders. The stagger is slight and the body lean is such that the weight is on the balls of the feet. The knees are in line with the feet, perhaps just a tad inside. They should not be exaggerated either in or out. The hands are on the knees with the thumbs on the inside and pointed down. If the head is up the rest of the body positions will fall in line.

A simple drill for checking the points of a good stance is to have all the candidates for the offensive backfield line up, one behind the other by positions. Have them assume the proper stance several times. Then use the starting cadence and have them all start together a few steps. Use both forward and lateral starts. Also, if your offense calls for shifting, use several shifts. The important thing in shifting is that the athlete ends up in a truly balanced stance; that is, his body weight is not leaning one way or the other.

**DIAGRAM #43**

## 2. LEAD BLOCKING DRILL

In most T or I formations, the running backs are called upon to execute the lead block. This is a running shoulder block and since it is always straight ahead, it requires great skill because the blocker (the running back) is usually not as strong as the defensive man he is called upon to block. He must use speed and momentum and position to get the job done. The blocker should always aim at the defender where the defender "bends" (his waist). He should not "pick a side" that he wishes to block. He should aim at the dead middle of the defender until the last split second and then quickly flick his head to the most logical side of the defender. If there is doubt, the blocker should not pick a side, but execute a block with his head straight into the defender's middle. It is most important that the blocker get under the hands or flipper of the defender. Often a slight dip just before contact will accomplish this. The blocker must maintain contact by determined leg drive so that the back with the ball may cut off his block.

The drill to teach this block is a mean one. It can be done by using a held standing dummy, but there is really no substitute for doing this one live. Place two markers—flat hand shields or towels or even standing dummies laid down—about two paces apart. Put a defensive man behind but between the markers. Align the lead blocker three yards from the defended "hole." On the starting signal, the blocker must blast the defender out of the hole. Do not allow the defender to cross the neutral zone. By adding a ballcarrier, a new dimension is added, but the basic drill is for the block.

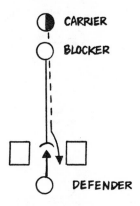

CARRIER

BLOCKER

DEFENDER

DIAGRAM #44

This same type of drill is so basic to blocking and hitting on defense that it can be used by the whole squad. If you are coaching a young team and you want to find out who your "hitters" are, this type of drill should be used. Line up eight or ten men in single file facing another file of about the same number. (Actually, numbers are not important. I have seen this drill done with the whole squad.) The markers are not important either. Just tell the defender to find the blocker, and vice-versa. The second man back in the blocking line carries the ball. The first defensive player is about five yards from the first blocker. On the hike, the blocker and defender seek contact with each other and the ballcarrier follows the blocker. As soon as they execute this, the defender goes to the end of the blocking line and the blocker goes to the end of the defending line. The ballcarrier flips the ball to the next man in the offensive line and lines himself up as the blocker next up. This is a fierce drill and everyone gets a crack at both offense and defense. When one player hits a particularly good lick, pull him out of the drill and "throw him a fish"—a piece of candy or a stick of gum. It usually doesn't take long to get everyone popping leather. It will quickly show you who your hitters are.

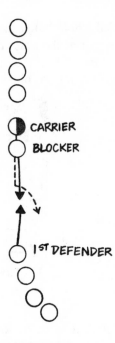

**DIAGRAM #45**

## 3. END BLOCKING DRILLS

Running backs must be able to block defensive ends (or linebackers stationed outside the offensive tight end) either in or out. Here again this can be done versus bags or people. The key coaching point is that the blocker must not show his intention to block either in or out. Today's defenders can "head read" so well that any indication by the blocker will cause a defensive reaction, which takes position away from the blocker. The block must approach straight away, the same as the lead block. If the block is a "kick out" block, the blocker slips his head to the inside at the latest possible moment and turns his backside to the hole. If the block is a "hook in" block, the blocker approaches the same, but at the last split second aims for the outside leg of the end and tried to achieve a crab block. If the defensive end's reaction is good, the blocker won't be able to achieve the "pin position" so he must continue to scramble for the outside leg. This keeps pressure on the defender and eventually will force him into a bad pursuit angle.

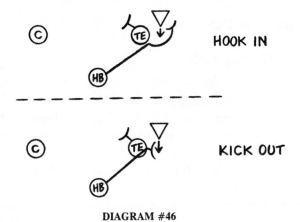

HOOK IN

KICK OUT

DIAGRAM #46

## 4. OPEN-FIELD BLOCKING DRILL

Use the same drills as described earlier.

## 5. PASS-BLOCKING DRILL

Set two running backs up in formations used in your passing offense. Have QB drop and set up at seven yards deep. Place a standing dummy (or other marker) at the extremities of the cup the linemen form. Bring a pass rusher outside the dummy. By making the two blockers step up and out, so that they block just outside the wall, you can work on their various techniques.

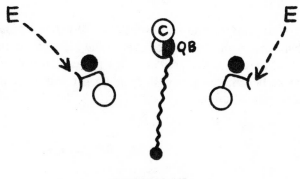

DIAGRAM #47

## 6. BALL-HANDLING AND HANDOFF DRILLS

### *Circle Warmup Drill*

Backs form a circle in groups of five or six. Use as many circles as possible. Give each group one football. Players are spaced about ten yards apart. They start running in the circle and throw the ball around in the circle, in any direction and to any man in the group. No player is allowed to return the ball to a player he received it from. Create competition by having each group complete as many passes as possible in a one-minute period. Everyone must keep going. No one may stop to catch the ball.

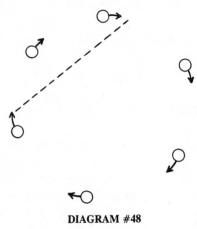

**DIAGRAM #48**

### *Running Forward Handoff Drill*

This is another warmup drill for backs. Divide the group equally, half as ballcarriers and half as receivers. The ball carriers run forward and hand off to receivers. Begin at a slow pace and finish at top speed. When backs become proficient at handing off and receiving, two or three balls may be used.

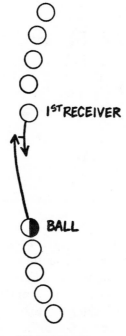

DIAGRAM #49

## Multiple Ball-Handling Drill

Divide the players into groups of eight. In each group, two lines of four players are placed so that they face each other. Number one hands off to number two, two to three, three to four, and so on until the end of the line. After each player has passed the ball, he stops at the position occupied by the player to whom he passed. Thus the formation is kept. When number eight receives the ball, he passes it back to seven, seven to six, six to five, etc. The first time around the ball should be handed to the next player as he goes by at full speed. The second time it should be flipped from a yard's distance. The third time around the receiver is three yards away from the flipper.

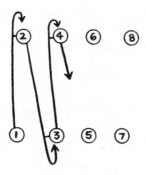

DIAGRAM #50

## Pitchout Drills

This drill is between the quarterbacks and the running backs. Quarterback and center take their normal alignment and the running backs take position of right and left halfbacks. The quarterback gives the starting signal, receives the ball from the center, and quick-tosses to the running back. They alternate first to the right then to the left side. The receiver must run a lateral banana route. The quarterback uses a one-handed, underhand spiral toss to the receiver. He steps out with a lead step to his left, if he is righthanded, and delivers the toss on the next step. However, in going to his right, he uses a reverse pivot in order to get into position to make a righthanded toss.

DIAGRAM #51

## Figure-Eight Ball-Handling Drill

Set three backs in row and give one of them a football. This is just like a basketball figure-eight drill. If the outside man has the ball, he tosses it to the middle man and cuts behind him. The middle man tosses it to the other outside man and then cuts behind him, and so on.

The secret is that the tosser always cuts behind the man he tossed to. When the backs become proficient at this drill and make their cuts quickly, the toss is reduced down to just a two-handed tap. Actually, the ball hardly looks like it is moving at all as the three backs weave down the field.

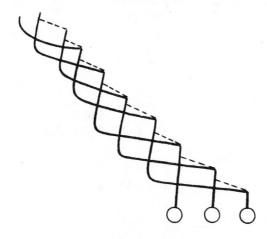

DIAGRAM #52

## Dive Drill

Place a quarterback, center and halfback in normal positions. In front of the running back, on the defensive side of the line of scrimmage, arrange any number of big bags on their sides. It should resemble a disordered stack of logs, some leaning on others. The starting cadence is given and the halfback runs the dive play. The quarterback receives the ball from the center and comes down the line of scrimmage laterally. He hands off to the diving halfback right on the line of scrimmage. The quarterback uses his inside arm and hand to place the ball in the arm pocket made for him by the running back. The running back doesn't look at the quarterback or the ball, but picks his route through the jumbled up dummies. It is the running back's job to pick the route after receiving the ball. The running back keeps his inside arm up, and outside arm down, forming a pocket. When he feels the ball in his belly, he brings his inside arm down and secures the ball. He must be a quick starter and be at top speed when he hits the line of scrimmage.

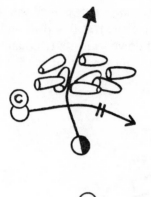

**DIAGRAM #53**

### 7. Faking Drills

It is difficult to practice faking individually. You need the interaction of the quarterback and at least two running backs. The key word is discipline. Fakers are not good fakers unless they can attract defenders. Here are five fundamentals of faking:

1. Run as low and as hard as when carrying
2. Always cant your body so your back is toward the point of attack
3. Carry on the fake at least five yards beyond the line of scrimmage
4. Have pride in the assignment
5. Ram the faking hole if cluttered

Set up the running backs with a quarterback. Have a defensive line of scrimmage and defensive linebackers holding standup bags or shields. The skeleton backfield runs the offense with emphasis on faking. Make defensive bag holders drive their bags (or shields) into the fakers.

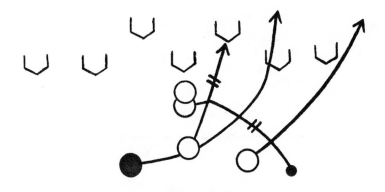

DIAGRAM #54

## 8. PUNT DRILLS—EXTRA-POINT DRILLS—CATCH DRILLS —ROUTE DRILLS—RELEASE DRILLS—TACKLING DRILLS

These drills are the same for backs as for the other positions described earlier.

## 9. CARRYING DRILLS

### *Gauntlet Drill*

Line up two lines of players with about eight or nine players in each line. Make the running backs run the gauntlet with the men in the two lines trying to snatch or pull the ball loose. The ballcarrier is allowed to use only one hand in carrying the ball in this drill. The same idea can be used when running skeleton running plays. Just have a couple of defensive linemen at the point of attack try to slap, pull or snatch the ball as the carrier hits the hole.

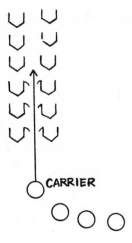

DIAGRAM #55

### Monkey Rolls with Footballs

This is the same tumbling drill that all the other team members use. The three men jump over and roll, keeping the three-men system going by being ready to jump over the rolling man as soon as they have completed their roll. The only thing that is different is that the backs carry footballs while executing this stunt.

### Run the Planks Drill

Use the same planks that are prescribed for the linemen, and use as many planks as needed. Have a man holding a dummy at the end of each plank. The backs run the planks and execute evasive action on the dummy. Use the stiff-arm, butt and pivot, head fakes, change the ball, etc.

DIAGRAM #56

### Burma Road Drill

Set up bags and bag holders five yards apart in a zig-zag course. Have the backs carry the ball straight at the first bag, where he executes a particular maneuver. The next bag is five yards further on at a 45° angle. When the runner arrives at the second bag, he uses a different maneuver. You should be able to train your ballcarriers to use five or six actions in one drill.

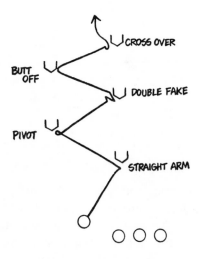

DIAGRAM #57

### Power Running Drill

Stack together about a dozen standing dummies without holders. Spare running backs align just outside the dummy formation to stand dummies back up when they are knocked down. Ballcarriers run at the dummies, plow through and attempt to blast them apart without losing their balance. Spare backs move up to running line and the ballcarrier who has just run takes his place in the line that straightens up the dummies.

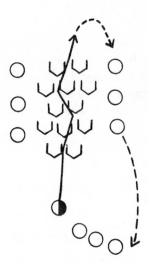

DIAGRAM #58

### Stiff-Arm and Sidestepping Drill

Station a man wearing full gear just beyond two standing dummies. Opposite him have a line of ballcarriers at least two of whom
should have footballs. The first man runs between the two dummies.
The defensive man shuffles into tackling position but does not tackle.
The runner uses his off arm to jolt the defender on the headgear or
shoulder pads as he executes his right or left break.

STANDING DUMMY

DIAGRAM #59

### *Dodge the Tire Drill*

Align two lines of players in single file with about seven or eight players in each line. The lines are five yards apart and the players are three to four yards behind each other. Each man has an automobile tire in a rolling position. The running backs run between the lines, one at a time, while the men with tires try to roll the tires at the back with the ball. The running back tries to keep from getting hit by the rolling tires. Another variation is to let the men with the tires throw the tires at the running back.

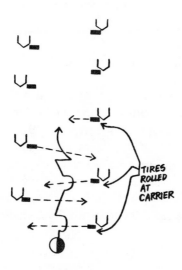

DIAGRAM #60

### *Helmet Run Drill*

Set up a center, quarterback and running back in formation. Go through regular cadence. Have five or six helmets beyond the line of scrimmage at intervals of five yards. Helmets are in a scattered formation. The ballcarrier is required to reach down and touch the helmets with his free hand. The stress is on speed and body balance. After all the running backs have completed the drill in one direction, turn the formation around and have them come back through again from the new direction.

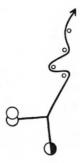

DIAGRAM #61

## Three-in-One Drill

This drill teaches three things: ball-handling, hard running, and proper carriage.

Set up with a quarterback, center and a line of running backs. Station two defensive linemen on the line of scrimmage. Behind them lay three standing dummies on their sides. Behind that have a line of tacklers. The regular cadence takes place and the running back receives the handoff and runs between the two defensive linemen. The linemen may make contact but may not tackle. The running back drives through and strides over the horizontal dummies. After he clears the last dummy, he must try to avoid the tackler.

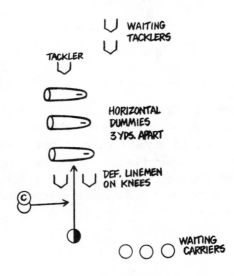

DIAGRAM #62

# E. FLANKER AND SPLIT END DRILLS

## 1. STANCE AND STARTS DRILLS

The wide receivers may use the drills for stance and starts that have been previously described for other offensive positions.

A general fundamental (both on offense and defense) is that the further you are from the ball, the higher the stance may be. Many wide receivers simply stand up with a slight foot stagger. Bear in mind that, as you bring this receiver in closer, his stance should become lower. When he aligns as a wing or flexed end, he should assume the same stance as a tight end.

*Coaching point on alignment of wide receivers.* You should always have a reason for the distance a wide receiver aligns from the formation. The first consideration is the defensive secondary plan you are facing. First, consider a defense facing you that is primarily a three-deep zone. You want to spread those three deep defenders to the maximum. In other words, make them have to cover the entire width of the field. If the receiver's route calls for at least ten yards' penetration into this zone, then your maximum split is nine yards from the boundary. If the route is a "quick" route, you may align closer to the boundary. Next consider a four-deep secondary, facing you, that is primarily a man-for-man with combinations on close together receivers. You want to align at seven yards from the main formation or from your next eligible receiver. This is because it is at this distance that the defensive men must decide on combination zone or straight man. Seven yards is a sort of twilight zone to the defense. If they play it "man," your crossing patterns will give them trouble. If they play it combination zone, they have stretched a two-man zone almost too far. If you align at six yards, they'll play zone easier and if you align at eight yards, they'll cover you man for man safely.

Of course, alignment is dictated at times by the pattern. Always bear in mind that the boundary is a defensive factor. When you align closer to the boundary than nine yards, you have restricted your maneuvers.

## 2. ROUTE DRILLS AND CATCH DRILLS

Route drills described under tight ends are also applicable for wide receivers. Here are a few extra drills.

### One-Handed Drill

This drill is very simple. In order to emphasize that receivers keep their eyes on the ball while receiving, have them catch with one hand only for a short period.

### Catch and Run Drill

Many receivers have a tendency to drift several yards after catching a pass without realizing that they should be heading for the goal line. Have a line of receivers run parallel to the line of scrimmage. Place two standing dummies just beyond the receiving area. The passer delivers the ball to the receiver just before he gets even with the two dummies. The receivers catch and break immediately between the two dummies and head for the goal line. Yardage is measured in only *one* way.

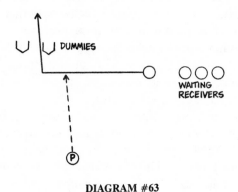

DIAGRAM #63

### Catch the Bomb Drill

Wide receivers line up in single file and run a streak or fly route. Passers hang the ball in front of them. Have a defensive back (or another receiver) run "hub to hub" along with the intended receiver; however, he should not make an attempt to deflect or catch the ball. This builds confidence in the receiver that the ball can be caught even though he is covered closely.

### One-on-One Games

This is a fun drill that both receivers and defensive backs like to play. Have a passer ready to throw whenever he thinks he can complete a pass to the offensive receiver. The offensive receiver is covered by a defensive back in a one-on-one situation. The receiver can run anything he wants to within a given time period. Start off with five seconds—from hike to ball release. Gradually increase the time. Don't hamper either the receiver or defender with too many rules. The idea is fun in an undisciplined situation. They will actually work harder the more relaxed the attitude becomes. This is just a change of pace drill and should not take up much of the organized practice schedule. Our players do this on their own sometimes before practice starts. Occasionally, some big linemen will try either end of this game and it usually provides for a good laugh from the others.

# F. QUARTERBACK DRILLS

### 1. STANCE DRILL

Begin by having all the quarterbacks in a line facing the coach. Do not use centers at first. Each quarterback assumes a parallel stance and flexes at the knees. He puts his hands out as if there were a center in front of him. The starting cadence is barked out in unison and each quarterback simulates taking the ball and then pulls both hands in to his middle.

### 2. EXCHANGE DRILL

Use the same format as in the stance drill but now add the center with a football. Points to stress: the quarterback placing his "take" hand firmly against the center's crotch; the back of this hand should exert pressure so the center can feel it; this hand should be fully extended but not rigid; the other hand is the cup hand and it also has fully extended fingers; the inside of both wrists should be touching.

Since the center always steps forward while bringing the ball up to the take hand, the quarterback must "ride" his hands forward while taking the ball. As soon as he has the ball firmly in both hands, he immediately brings both hands with the ball into his middle. Have all quarterbacks and centers do this together.

### 3. HANDOFF DRILL

These drills contain all the steps and pivots necessary to run the full running offense. There are many, many ways to teach these mechanical actions. Any marker can be used to limit the space and define the area. Such things as hurdles, helmets, tires, even towels can be placed in such a way that the quarterback must take proper steps. Prescribe every action so that they can be done "by the numbers." Example:

1. Hike and take
2. Lateral lead step
3. Opposite foot step
4. Inside hand forward with the ball
5. Second lead step
6. Second follow foot step
7. Hop and set
8. Fake set up for pass

The entire repertoire of plays can be executed by the numbers and all quarterbacks can do it together.

### 4. FAKING DRILL

Place managers or student assistants across the line of scrimmage aligned in defensive positions that should be affected by the offensive faking. Have the offensive running backs and quarterbacks execute the plays that involve faking (or hiding) the ball from those defensive positions. After each play, have the so-called judges grade their ability to see the ball.

### 5. DROP-BACK DRILL

This is very similar to the step-by-step drill used for running plays. It is most essential that the quarterback get back seven yards and set up in balance. Speed is also necessary. Teach the steps first, then go for quickness. There are two ways of getting back seven yards and setting up. One is to turn and sprint back with the head turned enough to see about half of the field ahead. The other way is to backpedal straight back which gives vision to the whole field. The first way is definitely faster but restricts the quarterback's vision. The second is slower but does have the whole ballgame in front of the quarterback's eyes. Either way, the quarterback must arrive at the proper spot and set to deliver the ball. Righthanded quarterbacks will have their right foot back. Their left foot should point to the direction of the throw. As the ball is delivered, a high release is desirable. The passing hand rotates counterclockwise so that after release the palm faces outside. If the pattern calls for a throw to either right or left, the feet must be changed, after setup, so that the lead foot always points toward the target.

## 6. PULL-UP DRILL

In the pull-up pass, the quarterback sprints to one side or the other, faking a full sprintout. When he is about even with his offensive tackle, he pulls up or stops. Normally he must bounce in order to get his feet in the proper position. What this does is move the pocket over about five yards. Since this maneuver often calls for a throw back to the other side, he almost has to change his feet 180°. After stopping, a quick hop will accomplish this—a maneuver which requires much practice.

## 7. SPRINTOUT DRILL

Again, like the previous quarterback action drills, the sprint requires precision and timing. Your priority is the first consideration. Are you going to sprint at containment with the idea of running if the containment breaks down and passing if it doesn't, or with idea of passing and then running only if everything else fails. Either way, you must put pressure on the container. Sprintouts are excellent if your passer is a short fellow. He can see better and doesn't get the ball batted down his throat.

Teach a few basic fundamentals. First, speed to the corner is important. Second, the quarterback must get turned upfield before passing. Tell him his navel must point toward the receiver and not the sideline. Third, never keep stringing out the play until you end up on the sideline. If the containment is good and nobody is open, lower your head and fight to find a crack in the pursuit. Hopefully you'll get back to the line of scrimmage. The sideline is the big loss and interception area. Fourth, don't retreat or go back against the grain unless the passer is also a very good runner.

## 8. THROWING DRILLS

### One Knee Passing Drill

An old and time-honored drill, this still remains the best way to teach arm and hand action. Simply have two passers play catch, both down on one knee.

### Target Passing Drill

Use a tire suspended from the crossbar on the goal-post. It will help if you have a net covering the area from the goal-post to the ground behind the tire. This saves a lot of shagging. Make the passer go through his steps before passing at the target.

### Clothesline Drill

To teach a high release and prevent sidearm passes, string a rope six feet high and have the passers pass to receivers at normal distances over the rope. As they become proficient, raise the height.

### Blitz Drill

Align three linebackers in normal positions. Set up with a center, quarterback, tight end, and running backs. Work on recognition with passer and receivers. When one, two, three, or none, blitz, the passer delivers the ball to the appropriate receiver releasing in the vacated linebacker area.

## 9. RECOGNITION DRILL

This drill can be done on paper, on the blackboard or by watching movies, but the best method is to set a full defensive perimeter in front of the quarterback. You train him to recognize defensive sets. There are two areas to be concerned with: keys before the snap, and keys after the snap. Keys before the snap are pretty simple. Three deep tells you zone right away. Most of the time it will be strong to your strong side, but a quick glance to the flanker side will confirm this. Four deep can reflect either man or zone, but watching the middle linebacker (or strong-side inside linebacker) after the snap, you can also tell. If he moves weak on your drop action, you are sure they are playing a zone.

You will want to present all types of defenses to your quarterback during your early-season training. Train him to know what offensive plays are best suited to run against the different formations. Here are a few tried and true axioms:

*1. Vs. wide tackle 6.* Run quick trap up middle, lead plays at the linebackers and sprint out with a short receiver in the flat.

*2. Vs. split 6.* Fold block both sides of the middle and run straight ahead; pass in the flats.

*3. Vs. 6-3.* Quick pass to tight end, three-man flood, trap.

*4. Vs. 5-4.* Trap, test the containment on sprintouts, five receivers out, three-man flood to strong side, either swing or flat.

*5. Vs. 5-4 Eagle.* Split line run lead blocking behind cross action, run at the middle.

*6. Vs. 4-3.* Close your formation and use power run against a seven front.

*7. Vs. 4-4.* Run wide.

# 3

# OFFENSIVE SEMI-GROUP, GROUP, AND TEAM DRILLS

## A. OFFENSIVE SEMI-GROUP DRILLS

### 1. CENTER AND GUARD DRILLS

You want to work with these two positions in two ways. Use a two-on-one situation and a two-on-two.

#### Two-on-One

Set up with the offensive center, either a right or left guard, and a defensive lineman opposing them. The defensive man aligns first over the center, but he should be moved from time to time to the gap or over the guard. You always need a ball and someone to take the snap. The regular starting signals should always be used and the coach should always have a whistle to end the action. Two-on-one blocking involves opening the hole, so turning the defender is more important than driving him straight back. On the snap, when the defender is over the center, the center executes a post block. This starts out like a fireout block. The center must stop the defender by getting his head into the defender's middle and maintaining contact. The guard steps off with his inside foot and aims his inside shoulder at the place where the defender bends. The guard drives with his outside foot. As soon as the center feels contact being made by the guard, he swings his hips into his own guard. He is on his all fours and continues pressure as he pivots. If the two men keep the seam closed and work together, they will easily turn the defender. The biggest error is when the two blockers get separated and the force of their drive actually goes against each other. The coach should stand behind the defender and give hand signals indicating a two-on-one block or a single block by the center while the guard pulls. Also, pass blocking can be mixed in.

Next move the defender to the gap and continue the same procedure. Of course, you must use spare blockers and defenders after every five blocks or so.

When the single defender is on the guard, the double-team assignments switch. The guard is now the post man and the center is now the turn man. Also, the fold block can be worked on in this situation. The center executes a turnout block and the guard opens up with his inside foot and pulls around (to the inside) the center's block.

CENTER POST          GUARD POST          GUARD FOLD
GUARD TURN           CENTER TURN

DIAGRAM #64

### Two-on-Two Drill

Use the same set up as just described, except add one more defender. The coach signals for both offensive men to execute right or left shoulder blocks, cross-blocks, fold blocks and pass blocks.

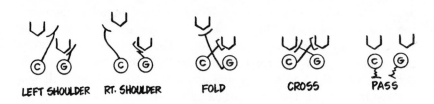

LEFT SHOULDER    RT. SHOULDER    FOLD       CROSS       PASS

DIAGRAM #65

## 2. GUARD AND TACKLE DRILL

Use the same drills as described for the center and guard. You will want to mix in more cross-blocking at these positions.

The cross-block is similar to the fold block. On the cross-block, the outside blocker fires out first and blocks down, while the inside blocker pulls and blocks out. This is the short trap. The puller doesn't actually open with his lead step, but merely takes a jab step. This step never points parallel to the line of scrimmage but points at the defender. When executed well, it almost looks like a hesitation by the inside man, allowing the down blocker to clear, and then a straight drive by the out-blocker. Neither blocker should ever raise up higher than their original stance.

TACKLE GOES
FIRST

DIAGRAM #66

The fold block is just opposite from the cross-block. The inside blocker fires across the line first and executes a turnout block. The outside blocker opens with his inside foot, giving the inside man time to clear and drives around this block to the inside. Usually fold blocks result in the outside man blocking on a linebacker.

GUARD GOES
FIRST

DIAGRAM #67

## 3. TACKLE AND END DRILL

These are also single blocks and double teams executed against one or two defenders—in other words, two-on-one or two-on-two. The tight end and tackle will double team more than any other line positions, so your work should be heavy with these two positions. When the tight end works with his tackle, he is always the turn man. Tight ends must learn to step off with their inside foot first and drive straight ahead on this first step. They turn on the second step. Their block is higher and they should not go to the ground with their hands. Their off-arm should pump in running action. A good blocking tight end is the cornerstone to a good running offense.

DIAGRAM #68

## 4. END AND WING DRILL

If your offense features a close wing, you must first perfect the double team between these two positions. When using the two-on-one drill, the techniques are the same as described before. The tight end is always the post and the wing is always the turn blocker. If your wing is a lightweight blocker, you are in the wrong formation. When you go to the two-on-two drill, the wing must perfect the reach block. Again, the coach can mix these blocks up by hand signals.

DIAGRAM #69

## 5. CENTER-TWO GUARDS DRILL

These drills are called "three-on-three." When working on this size group, every blocker must be signaled to by the coach or a huddle may be used. The whole middle attack is worked on against three defenders.

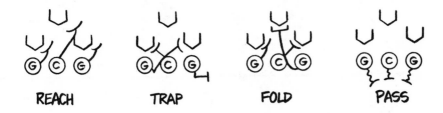

REACH          TRAP          FOLD          PASS

DIAGRAM #70

## 6. GUARD-TACKLE-END DRILL

This is also a three-on-three drill and is operated the same way as described above. All the single blocks, double teams and traps, cross-blocks and fold blocks and pass blocks can be perfected.

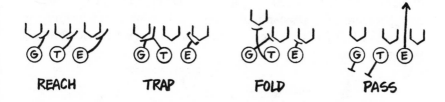

REACH          TRAP          FOLD          PASS

DIAGRAM #71

## 7. LINEMEN'S SEMI-GROUP DRILLS

### Board Drill

The planks, or boards, are the same ones described under individual drills. Instead of just an individual blocking the dummy down the plank, you now shoot for timing on the part of small groups such as center and guards, tackles and ends, etc.

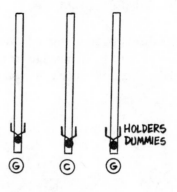

**DIAGRAM #72**

## Sled Drill

Use the two-man Crowther sled to work on two blockers perfecting their starts and blocking form. Also, two guards, back-to-back, can pull on cadence and block the sled simultaneously.

## Cage Drill

Everyone should have some form of training aid which makes linemen run low. If it is big enough, many drills can be done under this cage by small groups. Make sure the cage is not too low. Whenever your players "waddle" instead of run, you've got to raise the cage. Planks can be placed under the cage with held dummies just outside the cage perimeter. Guards can pull and trap and many linemen skills can be practiced. This is the best training aid you can have for training young linemen.

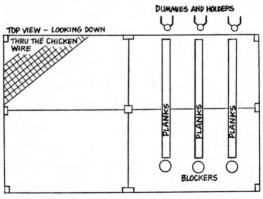

**DIAGRAM #73**

### Shoot Drills

The best way to describe the shoot drill is to say that it resembles the starting box in a horserace. The equipment must be constructed so that the spacing is proper and the height is not too low. Linemen practice starts from the shoots but can also use dummies and planks to work on blocking techniques as well.

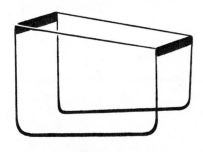

DIAGRAM #74

## 8. RECEIVER'S SEMI-GROUP DRILLS

### Two-on-Two Route Drill

Take two receivers who normally run patterns that compliment each other, such as split end and off-halfback, flanker and tight end, etc. Execute these routes against the appropriate defenders and execute crossing patterns, curl and flat patterns, and others. If possible, have two passers so that each receiver has an opportunity to catch on the same play.

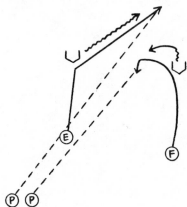

DIAGRAM #75

### Two-on-Two Blocking Drill

The same two receivers described above can work on the running game by executing their blocks. Since their blocks are wide open and done from a long running start, it is advisable to do this against dummies placed where the blocks should take place.

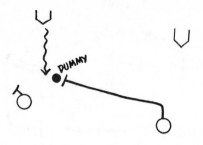

**DIAGRAM #76**

### Punt Coverage Drill

The two wide receivers are normally the two outside coverage men on punt plays. They should be drilled separately on this important phase. It is not necessary to have a punter or have the long sprint to get into position. Place a safety man in the middle of the field. On each side of him, about ten yards upfield, place two blockers. The two coverage men align ten yards in front of the blockers. The coach throws a high lob, the coverage men play off the blockers and cup the safety man. Stress speed in eluding the blockers, staying in lanes and coming to collection when approaching the tackle. The tackle is necessary, so it should be made live. This drill teaches position.

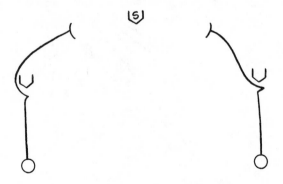

**DIAGRAM #77**

## 9. BACKS' SEMI-GROUP DRILLS

We covered some of these under individual drills such as faking drills, lead drills, etc. Here are a few more.

### Quarterback–Two Remaining Backs Drills

These are sometimes called skeleton drills. Use a piece of canvas for line positions. Stretch it out with markings for the offensive positions and spacings. The center passes to the quarterback and the three backs execute the offensive plays working on timing and ball-handling.

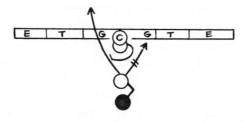

**DIAGRAM #78**

### Sprintout Drill

If the sprintout is going to be a part of your offense, you will want to do this drill frequently. Also, you must do it live until the lead blocker is an accomplished blocker.

Place two defensive containers (and spares) where they normally align. Run at them with two plays. The first is a kickout block by the near back and a run play inside of him. The second is a hook-in block and quarterback sprintout.

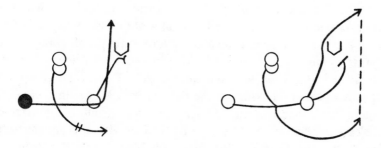

**DIAGRAM #79**

## 10. OKLAHOMA ALL GROUPS

This is the best semi-group drill in football. All offensive and defensive segments of the squad can benefit from the drill.

The basic structure is two markers placed seven feet apart. Anything can be used but the tall dummy laid on its side or held is the best because it keeps the runners inside the seven foot "hole." Place an offensive blocker in the middle of the area. Opposite from him place a defender right on the blocker's nose. They must be the length of the ball apart but can be as far apart as two yards in the case of a linebacker. A quarterback and center are placed so that the quarterback can hand off to a running back. The running back is three yards directly behind the blocker. The starting signal is given and the blocker attempts to block the defender out of the area between the bags. The quarterback hands off to the running back who cuts off the blocker's block. The defender attempts to ward off the blocker and tackle the back in or near the hole. Run this way, the drill slightly favors the offense if the personnel is equal. A great defensive play deserves much praise.

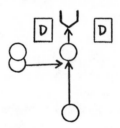

**DIAGRAM #80**

Using this same drill, the entire squad can work on this at one time. A good idea is to devote 15 minutes of the schedule just before a break and divide the whole team up into five groups, all going at once. The first group is the centers blocking on the middle linebackers with the fullbacks carrying, with one quarterback. The second group is the offensive guards blocking on the defensive tackles with a couple of running backs and one quarterback. The third group is the offensive tackles blocking on the defensive ends, also with appropriate backs. The fourth group features the tight ends blocking on the strong and weak linebackers; and last, the offensive wide receivers blocking on the defensive backs.

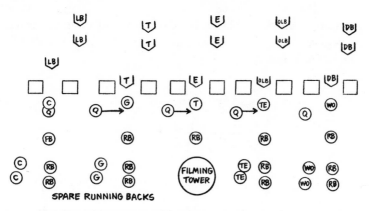

DIAGRAM #81

# B. OFFENSIVE GROUP DRILLS

## 1. MIDDLE DRILL

This drill encompasses the center, quarterback, two guards and fullback. Against them, on defense, have an even or odd line with one or two linebackers. Place two held dummies at the offensive tackle positions to mark the area. Concentrate running plays at this area.

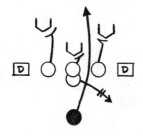

DIAGRAM #82

## 2. LEAD DRILL

Start with an offensive guard, tackle, center, quarterback and running backs. Against them have two defensive down linemen and one linebacker. Hold the dummies at the center's nose and at the tight end position to mark the area. Run mostly lead (sometimes called isolation) plays but mix in traps, draws, handoffs and cross-blocks to keep the defense honest.

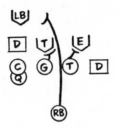

DIAGRAM #83

### 3. OFF-TACKLE DRILL

You need a center, quarterback, guard, tackle, tight end and running backs. Against them, you put two defensive linemen, one of whom is the container. The offense runs off-tackle plays. Be sure you block this different ways. Mix in kickout blocks between the near back (or fullback) and the guard or tackle. Mark the area with dummies.

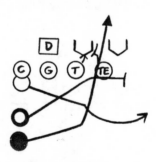

DIAGRAM #84

### 4. SWEEP AND OPTION DRILL

You need a backfield, tight end, quarterback and center. Place one defender on the tight end, and use a cornerback and strong safety. Run sweeps and options. Use dummies to mark the area. Pass plays can be mixed in to keep the defense honest.

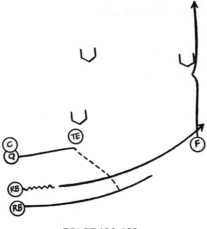

DIAGRAM #85

## 5. BULL IN THE RING

This is really a carrying drill, but all backs are involved so we place it under group drills. Form a ring of tacklers of six or eight players around a back with the football. The back can hit any area in any way, but his goal is to break the ring. A penetration of three yards beyond the ring is usually pretty good.

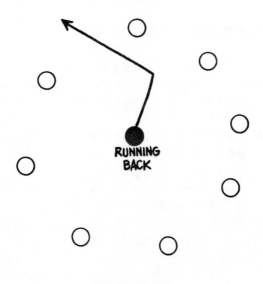

DIAGRAM #86

## 6. SKELETON PASS DRILLS

When you involve all your backs and ends against a full perimeter of defense, you concentrate on the passing game. An occasional draw or sweep may be used, but this set up is primarily to perfect the pass offense.

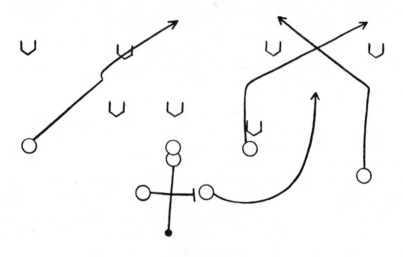

DIAGRAM #87

## 7. FIVE INTERIOR LINEMEN DRILL

Whenever the backs and ends are working on the skeleton pass drills, the schedule must provide for a group drill involving the remaining five interior linemen. They can work on pass blocking or interior run plays.

A good pass-blocking drill is to work two offensive lines, alternating every five plays, against five defensive rushers. Use a spare quarterback (a manager or wounded player will do) who takes the ball from center and sets up but does not pass. The coach or other manager uses a stopwatch, which he starts on the snap of the ball. The watch is stopped when the player with the ball is tagged. After five plays, the time is added up. For example, say the first line held off the rushers for 25 seconds. The next line now has their five shots and they try to beat the 25-second record. This is highly competitive and really makes each blocker do his best. The defense should be changed every ten plays.

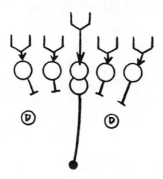

DIAGRAM #88

## 8. HALF LINE DRILLS

Divide the offense into two groups. The first group is the strong-side people: tight end, strong tackle, strong guard and center. They have a full backfield and they scrimmage against half a defense. Of course, they work on the whole strongside attack, runs and passes. At another place on the field, the weakside people do the same thing. This group has a center, a backfield, a weak (sometimes called ''quick'') guard and tackle and a split end. All the weakside plays are run against half a defense. This sort of scrimmage gets twice as much done as regular scrimmage because there never is an ''off'' side.

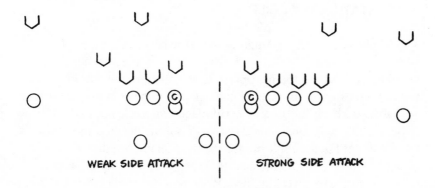

WEAK SIDE ATTACK          STRONG SIDE ATTACK

DIAGRAM #89

## C. OFFENSIVE TEAM DRILLS

### 1. HASHMARK DRILL

These drills can be done dummy or live but the purpose is to run the offense from hashmark to hashmark. Start on one hashmark and run a play; the next play is in the middle; the third is on the other hashmark. Have a coach or manager move the ball each time.

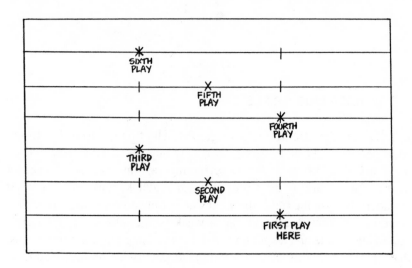

DIAGRAM #90

### 2. STATIONARY DRILL

There is a need for running the offense in one place. Use two huddles. One team breaks and runs a play while the next team is huddling and calling the next play. In this fashion the coaches can all watch both offenses at once. It enables you to have enough assistants available to check the line of scrimmage and each position. The defense should carry hand shields or wear aprons because they must be mobile to get lined up in time for the next team. Another wrinkle can be used here. When running pass plays, have spare quarterbacks throw passes to all the receivers at once. Receivers can never catch too many balls. The team quarterback throws to the primary receiver. The three spare quarterbacks throw to an assigned receiver.

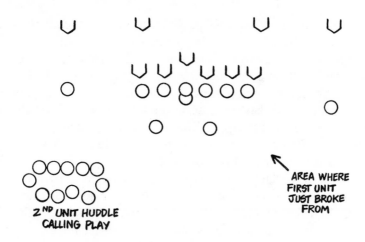

2<sup>ND</sup> UNIT HUDDLE
CALLING PLAY

AREA WHERE
FIRST UNIT
JUST BROKE
FROM

DIAGRAM #91

### 3. UP AND DOWN THE FIELD DRILL

When not scrimmaging, it is a good plan to move the ball forward five yards each play as well as from hash to hash. This gives the quarterback choices in the different areas of the field, from three-down zone to four-down zone and goal line. Also, punts and field goals can be worked in. This can be down against a dummy defense, scrimmage or against the wind. It is a particularly good drill for the day before the game. It is really a dress rehearsal.

### 4. LIVE DUMMY

Coaches for years have sought the solution to working an offense against a defense that reacts positively while avoiding injury. The answer is the live-dummy drill. The defense is live to fight blocks but is not allowed to tackle. This prevents pileups and avoids injuries. It isn't easy to control. It takes real good coaching. The defense must be content with reaction to position and then "pull the string." Actually it is a good drill for both offense and defense.

### 5. SCRIMMAGE

There comes a time when everyone must lay their ears back and put an offense against a defense full tilt. The object is to make ten yards in three or four plays. If possible, the chains should be on the field and there should be officials (or acting officials). All the coaches should get behind the offense and films should be taken, if the budget allows. Different areas of the field should be considered. The day should end with a real goal-line party. It is really tough to put your best offense against your best defense in this area because one-half your team isn't going to be happy. This can be avoided if you put the number one offense against the number two defense and vice-versa; but you lose some of the fire when you do this.

One more coaching point regarding offense: defensive linemen and linebackers are born; offensive linemen are made. Offense requires skill; defense requires frenzy. Everyone must have togetherness and morale, but without training and mastery of technique, you will never have a great offense.

# 4

# INDIVIDUAL DEFENSIVE DRILLS

## A. INTERIOR LINEMEN

### 1. STANCE DRILL

Regardless of the defensive front used, certain positions are always "down-linemen." They are the front-line troops, and although their stances may vary, there are certain basic fundamentals to be followed. Keep in mind the axiom, "The closer to the ball, the lower the stance."

Place a football on a yard line. Line up your defensive front (four or three) spaced normally off the ball. Behind them are candidates for the same position. The first group gets on one knee. Have a player (manager or coach) approach the ball as the offensive center. When he puts his hands on the ball, the defensive front men move into their stance. When the ball is pulled, the defensive men charge forward a few yards.

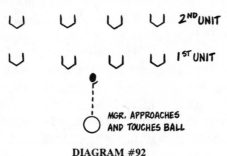

DIAGRAM #92

113

*Some coaching points on the stance by down-linemen:*
Down-linemen should always start from the position of one knee on
the ground. This is the position they seek after they break the defensive
huddle. There is a reason for this beside the brief rest. Linebackers and
safeties must recognize offensive sets and very often must react
quickly to get lined up, especially if they flip-flop. There is nothing
tougher than trying to see through four big linemen who are standing
up. The time to go into the defensive stance is when the offensive
center puts his hands on the ball. He is the only man who can start the
play so he's the player who everyone on defense should use as a ready
signal. From the one-knee-down position, it is very easy to hop into a
four-point (or three-point) stance. First the defensive player should be
on the knee of the foot that will be staggered back. He then reaches out
with the hand and arm on the same side as the leg that is down. From
this position, he simply makes a small hop to bring the other foot back
and the other hand down. This stance is easy to get into. Fundamentally, it is similar to the offensive stance, but it is a little lower. The
feet can be too wide or staggered too much. The shorter the man, the
narrower the base should be. Make sure the tail is not higher than the
head. Of course, the head is up and set down into the shoulders. In the
case of 4-3 ends or 5-4 tackles, a three-point stance is often preferred.
It is a little higher and affords a little better vision. When they are not
flanked by an end within five yards, they should go to a two-point
stance because they usually act as a container in this situation.

## 2. FIRST-STEP DRILLS

The first step of the defensive charge is most important to down-
linemen. Usually, it is also a hitting step; that is, contact is usually
made on the first step. This first step can be practiced against a sled, a
dummy, a shiver board or another player. In teaching young players, it
is best to start out hitting another player, using the first step only.

Take your line group and divide them into single lines of five
each. The first man in line turns around and faces the next man in line
and gets down on all fours. He keeps his head and shoulders high.
Each man in line comes up, one at a time, and executes his stance and
fires forward one step—and only one step. He strikes a blow either
with his "flipper" or hand shiver. If he is hitting with a flipper, he hits
one side of the man on his knees. He drives his shoulder pad into the
shoulder pad of the down man and brings up his arm to strike the blow.
All this happens on one step. Make him hold his position so he can be

corrected. The sequence goes like this: uncoil the legs, drive the shoulder and bring up the flipper and take a short jab step on the side you are hitting with. It is all part of one motion—foot and forearm. When this becomes natural, the defensive man should be able to strike a very hard blow. It must be strong enough to stop the offensive blocker's charge because reaction off the block comes next and the blocker must be neutralized and not into the defender's body. If the defender is hitting with a two-hand shiver, he drives both hands into the blocker's pads. He must keep his elbows in and hands close together. The wrists are locked and the defender must be ready to run. The reason for being at arm's length is quick escape.

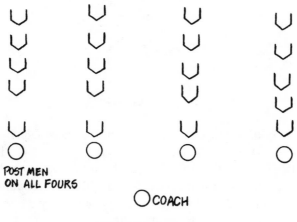

DIAGRAM #93

## 3. REACTION DRILLS

Defense is reaction to the offense's action. There are many reaction drills and most of them can be done by all positions on defense. In order to keep from drawing up drills twice or three times, there will be a reference back to the first description of the particular drill, when it is applicable to other defensive positions.

### Head-Reading Drill

All defensive men in the vicinity of the line must be able to "read" blockers. The best setup is one-on-one at about half speed. The offensive blocker should be controlled by the coach who stands behind the defensive lineman. Arm and hand signals indicate a reach block, turnout block, pull, down block (trap), or pass block. The defensive man reacts to each action by an appropriate defensive action. Examples:

*1. Reach block*—indicates an outside run or pass. Defender uses a hand shiver as soon as he sees the blocker turn his head and shoulders to the defender's outside. The hand shiver is adequate to keep the blocker out of the defender's body as this is not a power block. When the defender has the blocker at arm's length, he shuffles laterally to the outside, always keeping his outside leg back and free.

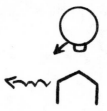

**DIAGRAM #94**

*2. Turnout block*—indicates an inside run. Defender should meet this block with a shoulder and flipper as it usually is a power block. After contact, the defender may have to drop step with the foot he made the initial step with, provided he still keeps forward pressure. He then drives to the inside, keeping his shoulders square to the line of scrimmage as he locates the point of attack.

**DIAGRAM #95**

*3. Pull*—indicates a wide play, which will be accompanied by a down block from an offensive player aligned outside the defender. Or, it is set up for an inside out trap. This key is the most difficult of all because the two options are opposed. The defender should brace his outside shoulder and leg first. If the down block is coming, it will come right now, and can be met with outside shoulder and flipper. Escape depends upon how well the down blocker has shut off the pursuit route. A good jolt and lateral slide is sometimes enough. If the blocker had great position, there are only two avenues left: one is the pivot to the outside; the other is to take the inside route. The inside route is dangerous because the defender is forced into an inside arc pursuit angle, but sometimes quickness can re-establish pursuit angle. If the down block is not forthcoming, the defender should shuffle laterally to the inside, keeping square and looking for the inside-out trap. Men positioned over the offensive guards can get help on this tough key. They should keep the center in their vision. If he blocks counter to the guard pull, the defender should always play trap first.

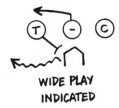

WIDE PLAY
INDICATED

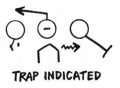

TRAP INDICATED

**DIAGRAM #96**

*4. Down block*—Whenever the "key" blocks down on the man inside the defender, the defensive reaction is always inside. Simply close the hole laterally without penetration.

CLOSE
LATERALLY

**DIAGRAM #97**

*5. Pass block*—On pass block show, the defensive lineman must immediately drive forward, knowing he must pressure the passer, but he must also be aware of the possibility of draw. The best way to keep the defensive linemen after the passer without fear is to keep them driving straight through the blocker until they see the quarterback get deeper than the running backs. Then they can go around blockers and get back into rushing lanes. As long as they are square with the blocker, they can react to the draw, but once the quarterback passes deeper than the running backs, the draw worry is over.

There are a couple noteworthy coaching points regarding pass rush. First, when the blitz is on, the rusher does not do all the "reading" described above; he drives over blockers and uses his shoulders and flipper to meet the pop and recoil. When reading, the rusher keeps boring in but should use his hands to keep the blocker at arm's length. It's just fundamental that you can't maneuver when the blocker has body contact with you.

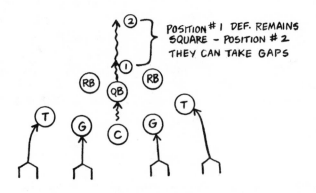

**DIAGRAM #98**

### Half-Circle Drill

This is one of the best drills to teach reaction. Place a defensive lineman in front of three blockers cupped around him. Use as many groups of four as you need. This is a rotation drill. When the defender finishes, he moves into the blocking cup and one of the blockers takes his place out in front. Give the three blockers numbers such as one, two and three. On the ready signal, the defender gets into a hitting position (the basketball guard position) and quickly moves his feet in place. The coach calls out any number between one and three. The blocker whose number is called moves forward quickly and sticks a shoulder at the defender. The defender steps into the blocker and strikes a shoulder flipper blow and bounces back into position. The coach quickly calls another number and so on. The defender learns he cannot turn to meet the blocker or he'll never get back in time to meet the next one. This keeps him square to all three blockers and teaches him to hit with either side.

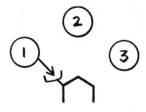

DIAGRAM #99

### Ricochet Drill

Place four players in single file. The first three are designated as blockers and the fourth one is the ballcarrier. A fifth man faces the first blocker in a hitting position. He is the defender you are working on. At a given signal the first blocker charges the defender and strikes a shoulder blow in his right or left shoulder. As soon as he bounces off, the next blocker, who is already in forward motion, strikes a shoulder blow on the opposite shoulder of the defender. The last blocker follows and hits back on the original shoulder. The defender hits each blocker with a one step, shoulder and flipper pop and quickly regains hitting position for the next blocker. After the defender has shed the last blocker, he puts a square tackle on the runner.

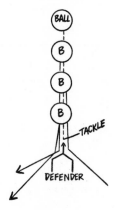

DIAGRAM #100

### Aping Drill

This is done in groups of three. Two men face one, all on their hands and knees. The one man is the first mover, the other two try to do everything the one player does. The man who is "it" jumps, rolls, crabs, fakes and anything he can as quickly as he can in order to lose the two who are trying to "ape" him.

### Aping and Tackle Drill

Use the same setup as above, the only difference being that the first mover is now a ballcarrier. When he succeeds in getting the two defenders fairly far apart, he tries to run between them. A good place to do this is on the two-yard line. It gives the "ballcarrier" a line to shoot for. Your best defenders should be able to follow all the movements and meet the ballcarrier, shoulder to shoulder, closing the gap between them.

### Big Sled Piano Drill

Take all the defensive linemen to the big seven-man sled. Line them up in single file. The first man in line starts out by hitting the first upright with a two-hand shiver. He bounces to the next upright and does the same thing, and so on down the line. As soon as the first man is two uprights down the line, then the next man in line starts the procedure and so on until all the men have gone through using the shiver. Next have them go through using the flipper and finally they go through the line using a flipper, pivot and roll. They hit every other upright when rolling.

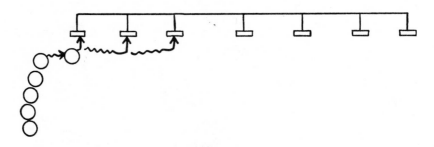

**DIAGRAM #101**

### Reaction and Footwork Drill

Take the defensive linemen to an area where you have seven

standing dummies, on their sides, lined up in a row. The dummies are just one yard apart. The linemen line up by the side of the first dummy. You need another line of B-teamers or JVs to act as ballcarriers; however, footballs are not needed in this drill. The B-teamers come up one at a time and face the defensive lineman who is next in line. At a starting signal, the B-teamer runs laterally above the line of dummies. The defensive man must face him all the way while running laterally *over* the dummies. The B-teamer stops, starts and reverses his field. The defender must always face him. This teaches lateral movement, over obstacles, without looking at the feet, and it makes the defender pick up his feet as he shuffles laterally.

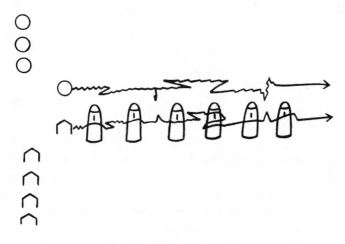

DIAGRAM #102

### *Reaction and Fumble Recovery Drill*

Use a one-on-one situation with the coach standing low behind the blocker. The coach has a football. On the hike, the defender wards off the blocker and the coach rolls the ball to either side. The defender must shed the blocker and fall on the ball.

DIAGRAM #103

### Two-on-One

Place a defensive lineman in front of two blockers. The coach stanɑs behind the defender and gives hand signals to the blockers. On the hike, the blockers may single block, down block, pass block, double team or split, indicating trap. The defender reacts to defeat each situation.

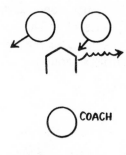

DIAGRAM #104

### Three-on-One

This is the same sort of drill but by adding one more blocker, the down block may come from either side. Stress the idea that the defender is at the apex of a triangle and must have both outside blockers in his vision. If the defender seems to be unable to react quickly enough to defeat the double team from either side, have him back off the line of scrimmage a little farther. This will give him more reaction time and will also enable him to see the outside men better.

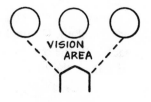

DIAGRAM #105

### Four-on-One

This is the same drill as above but adds a live trapper. You may now present just about all situations on a full-speed basis.

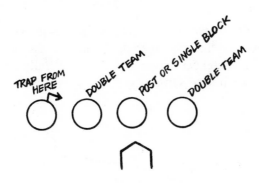

DIAGRAM #106

## 4. PASS-RUSH DRILL

The individual pass-rush drill is a one-on-one situation. The blocker shows pass on the snap and the defensive man executes his pass-rush techniques. The coach sets the situation. He tells the defender it is either a "read" or "press" defense. Be sure the blocker uses the type of pass blocking that relates to what the defender will be facing in the game. Also, have an extra blocker pick up the rusher after he escapes the first blocker when in the "reading" situation. Very often on "reads" you will only have four rushers, which allows the offense extra blockers. Your rusher must fight through two, sometimes three blockers to get to the passer.

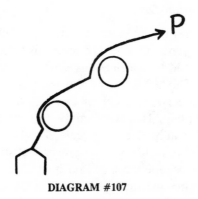

DIAGRAM #107

## 5. PURSUIT DRILL

Have the defender hit a dummy or stationary blocker and take the proper pursuit angle to a ballcarrier. The ballcarrier runs inside and outside and wide either way. Have the ballcarrier cut back some. Teach the defender the proper angle to take to assure interception. Also, be sure the defender learns how to run laterally with his shoulders square to the line of scrimmage.

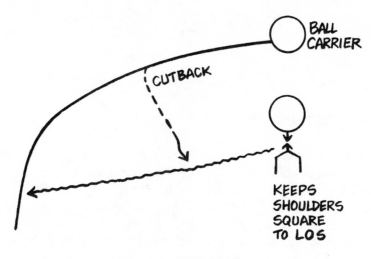

DIAGRAM #108

## 6. TACKLING DRILLS

### Dummy Position Drill

Have two lines of defenders in single file, the lead men facing each other at five yards. Designate one line as ballcarriers and one line as tacklers. The lead ballcarrier runs about half speed at a 45° angle from the tackler. The tackler paces him and shuffles into him, keeping square. At the precise moment of contact, the ballcarrier lifts his weight by a slight hop. This is a dummy drill and features a minimum of real contact. It can be done in sweats. The lifting by the ballcarrier enables the tackler to tackle without power, but still get the effect of a driving lift. It teaches footwork and position. The ballcarrier is not put on the ground. After the lift, the ballcarrier goes to the tackling line and the tackler goes to the carrier line. Everyone should get a couple of angle tackles each way.

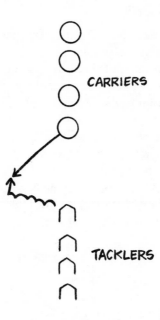

DIAGRAM #109

## Open-Field Tackling Drill

Use two chalk lines three yards apart and about ten yards long. Place a ballcarrier behind one line and a tackler behind the other. On the starting signal, the ballcarrier can use any maneuver he wishes, but he tries to cross the line defended by the tackler. The tackler is free to go after the ballcarrier in any fashion as long as he prevents the three-yard gain. This teaches open-field tackling without the problem of injury because at three yards neither player can get up too much of a head of steam.

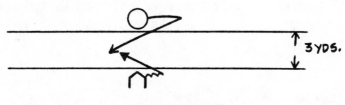

DIAGRAM #110

## Inline Tackling Drill

Young linemen need this. When a boy first comes out for football and is assigned a defensive line position, he is not really sure he can tackle anyone. When most of the drills feature warding off a blocker first, it becomes sort of a security blanket for the youngster to just get blocked, thereby avoiding the unknown of inline tackling. This drill will build his confidence.

Set up two hand shields seven feet apart. Put a blocker between them but put him on his hands and knees and tell him to absorb the defender's charge without moving. Now run the ballcarrier either side of the stationary blocker but between the hand shields. The defender is now almost forced to make a tackle. Once he finds out he did it and didn't get hurt, he'll be eager to escape blockers so he can do it again.

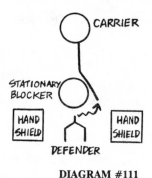

DIAGRAM #111

## Scramble Tackling Drill

Take a line of ballcarriers and face them with a line of tacklers. The first two men in each line come forward and lie on the ground on their backs. Their heads point to each other at a distance of about three yards. Put a football on the ground in front of the player designated as carrier. On a starting signal, they both scramble to their feet. The carrier picks up the ball and tries to avoid the tackler. The tackler tries to put the carrier down as soon as possible. Players switch lines after each play.

BALL CARRYING
LINE                                                    TACKLING LINE

DIAGRAM #112

### Sideline Tackling Drill

Station the ballcarriers in a line single file, to come up one at a time. Have an equal number of tacklers on defense in a line facing the carriers at 15 yards. Both lines are on the hashmark. On the starting signal, the carrier runs toward the sideline. The tackler closes in on the runner. The runner can use any maneuver to avoid the tackle except a cutback. This will teach the defender the value of the sideline.

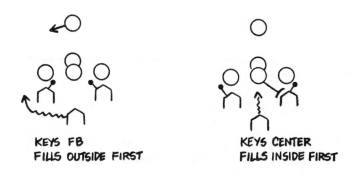

KEYS FB
FILLS OUTSIDE FIRST

KEYS CENTER
FILLS INSIDE FIRST

DIAGRAM #113

## B. LINEBACKERS

### 1. STANCE DRILL

Stances for linebackers vary depending on the style of defense being used. The big difference is in the feet, but in general, all inside linebackers should have their feet even without much stagger. Outside linebackers should have their outside foot back. All linebackers should learn a basic body position that is known as the hitting position. This position features forward body lean, straight back and knees flexed. Both arms are straight down with hands just inside the knees. Any outside linebacker will have three basic positions on a tight end. He will be just outside a tight end who is in a normal alignment. The expression "ear to ear" means the linebacker's inside ear should be even with the tight end's outside ear. The linebacker will be head-on if the tight end flexes two yards from the offensive tackle. Finally, the linebacker will be on the tight end's inside shoulder if the tight end flexes up to five yards. After five yards, the linebacker can either come back and keep a two-yard spacing with his end or walk off. Walk off means he backs off the line of scrimmage two yards and splits the difference between the split end and the offensive tackle. When the linebacker is normal, he has his outside foot back. When head on, his feet are parallel. When inside, the linebacker drops his inside foot back.

Because of these variances, stance drills should be done against JV players in a variety of tight and split formations. One basic tip for middle linebackers: never get up inside the stance of your tackles.

### 2. FIRST-STEP DRILL

Linebackers should do the first-step drill as outlined under interior defensive linemen.

### 3. REACTION DRILLS

Linebackers also do the reaction drills as previously outlined, but here are a few that are peculiar to linebackers.

#### Middle Linebacker Reading Drill

Middle linebackers and defensive tackles hold down four defensive holes. They can not do this unless they constantly work some kind of deal. Two basic ways to do this are to have a call for the tackles to be assigned the two outside holes while the middle linebacker takes the two inside holes and vice-versa. When assigned the two outside holes, the middle linebacker keys (reads) the fullback or number three eligible on the strong side. He must fill outside his tackles on all run plays. He is vulnerable to counters so this should be mixed with the tackles assigned the outside holes and the middle linebacker assigned the two inside holes. On this situation, the middle linebacker keys the offensive center. Because of this, the middle linebacker and two tackles should work together on reading drills. Also, some reaction drills can be done by the middle linebacker alone.

Mark the offensive holes with dummies or towels. Use the middle linebackers one at a time against a center and fullback. When keying the fullback, the middle linebacker fills the proper hole on a one-step key. The same is done with the center. These are not stunts but just the basic way to play the 4-3. When the offensive center checks back either way, the middle linebacker has to fill right now. He must react to reach blocks, guard slip blocks and even tackle-through blocks. He must also react to pass.

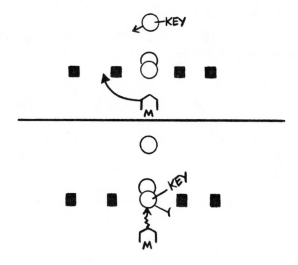

DIAGRAM #114

### Outside Linebacker Reading Drill

Outside linebackers are either on a tight end or on a split end side. Most teams flip-flop, so one linebacker is always on the tight end and the other is always on the split end side. However, the weak linebacker must learn to play against a weak tight end. As such, both must read reach blocks, turnout blocks, down blocks, etc.

Every day these linebackers face these keys put on by JVs or B-teamers and react until the reaction becomes instinctive.

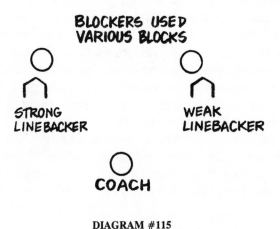

DIAGRAM #115

### Half-Circle and Ricochet Drills

All linebackers should do these drills as described in the section under defensive interior linemen.

### Ward-Off Drill

Line up a tight end. Put a linebacker on his outside shoulder. Also line up three more blockers in an I-formation one yard off the line of scrimmage and one yard to the inside of the tight end. On the starting signal, the tight end reach blocks on the linebacker. As the linebacker shuffles out, the other three blockers run at him. The first blocker tries to roll him up and as soon as the linebacker sheds him, the next blocker throws, and so on across the field.

DIAGRAM #116

### 4. PASS-RUSH DRILL

Linebackers rush the passer on presses only. They must learn the route they take and how to drive through blockers. Every defense unit should have an area of the field off in a corner with large posts sunk in the ground. These posts represent offensive line positions. Some schools even put old shoulder pads and headgear on top of the posts to further simulate offensive blockers. Usually there are six posts about a yard apart from tip of shoulder pad to tip of shoulder pad. By moving a football in front of certain posts, you can make the split end side either side. Defensive unit can use this area to work on hole assignments, blitz routes, etc. When working on linebacker blitzes, have them fire through the proper hole. Also, you can place a live blocker in back of the post line to provide training in driving past a live blocker after the linebacker has cleared the rush hole.

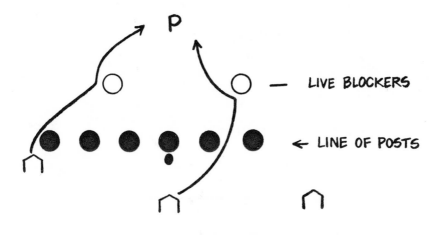

LIVE BLOCKERS

LINE OF POSTS

DIAGRAM #117

### 5. PASS DRILLS

Linebackers need a lot of work in breaking on the ball and catching the ball. Most of their work on position, stance, etc., is covered under semi-group drills, but here are a few individual drills against the pass.

#### *Catch Drills*

Linebackers align in single file and run toward the passer. First he throws high lobs and they try to catch the ball at the highest possible point in the trajectory. Then the linebackers break off and run at an angle. The passer throws lead passes. Next they should have some tip drills. Just about everyone runs some form of tip drill. A good way to assure a tip that is consistent is for the tipper to use another football. By holding the second ball tightly and striking the pass, the tipper gets a better tip than by using his own hands.

#### *Individual Zone Drill*

Use a center and a quarterback and one linebacker. On snap, the linebacker reads pass, turns and runs back to his area, looking at the passer over his shoulder. At a prescribed number of steps, he comes to collection and squares up. At this point, the quarterback throws the ball in his vicinity. The linebacker breaks on the ball and catches it.

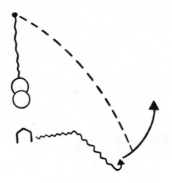

DIAGRAM #118

### Individual Man Coverage Drill

Take the strong linebackers and have them cover a tight end or fullback one-on-one, using mostly short routes. Stress keeping the eyes on the receiver. Teach backpedaling and pick up on the receiver's break. Weak linebackers work against a back coming out of the back-field. They keep a safe distance and stay as wide as the receiver, breaking up when the ball is thrown. The reason is that if their man runs a flat-and-up, they can turn and run with him.

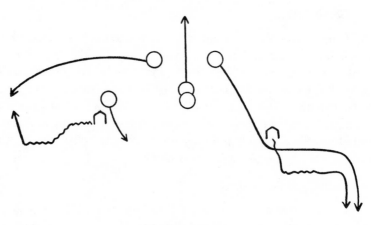

DIAGRAM #119

## 6. PURSUIT DRILL

The biggest mistake linebackers make is committing too soon. Middle linebackers must learn to bounce in place until sure of route to take to the ballcarrier. Outside linebackers have an axiom, "When in doubt, shuffle out." Stress these things when teaching pursuit angles. Run cross fakes and counters as well as tear sweeps. In each case, check the individual pursuit route. Make sure they understand what leverage on the ball means.

## 7. TACKLING DRILLS

Again, linebackers use many of the tackling drills explained earlier under defensive interior linemen. Here are a couple that are exclusively linebacker specials.

### Eye-Opener Drill

Use four markers two yards apart. They can be dummies or shields. Have a line of ballcarriers on one side of the markers and a line of linebackers on the other side. On the starting signal, the first ballcarrier runs for the three holes created by the markers. He may hit the first hole wide open or he may fake it and hit another hole. He may feint at all three and hit back to number-one hole. The linebacker who is up shuffles square and keeps leverage on the ball. As soon as the ballcarrier commits, the linebacker tackles him with a square tackle. Angle tackles are better than no tackles, but the linebacker seeks to stop the ballcarrier dead without forward progress.

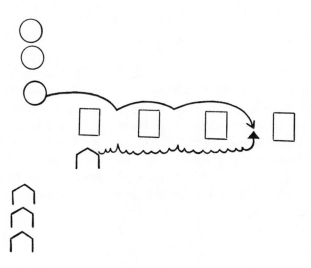

DIAGRAM #120

## *Defensive Version of the Running Shoulder Block Drill*

This drill was described under offensive drills, but it is essential to linebackers. Place the markers seven feet apart. Line up a running blocker with a ballcarrier behind him at two yards from the markers. Place the linebacker two yards from the markers on the other side. At the starting signal, the running blocker and linebacker meet in the hole. The linebacker tries to destroy the block, escape and make the tackle. This drill can be enlarged to widening the gap to 14 feet and using two blockers and two linebackers with one ballcarrier.

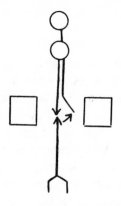

DIAGRAM #121

## *Goal Line and Short Yards Tackling Drill*

Many offensive backs are successful in vaulting over a cluttered line for a necessary yard or two. The way to defense this maneuver is for one or two linebackers to meet the vaulter in mid-air.

Take a number of big dummies, hand shields, etc., and make a pile seven yards long and about 30 inches high on the two-yard line. Put two linebackers behind the pile. Have two running backs on either side of the quarterback in position to take a quick handoff. The center snaps to the quarterback and he runs a handoff to either of his backs. The back who gets the ball vaults over the pile. The two linebackers will get to where they can meet him shoulder to shoulder.

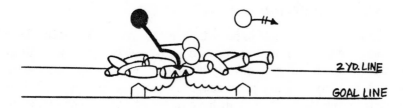

DIAGRAM #122

## C. SECONDARY INDIVIDUAL DRILLS

### 1. STANCE DRILL

The farther you are from the ball, the higher the stance should be. Secondary backs use a slightly higher version of the linebacker stance. They want to be like a basketball guard. Such things as hands on knees or hips are no good because then you must move up or down before you can move in a certain direction. Secondary people must be ready to move without lost motion. Safetymen use a parallel stance, cornerbacks and halfbacks generally use the outside foot back. If a cornerback is playing man coverage on a wide receiver, he should align in such a way that he takes something away from the receiver. If he lines up directly head-on, he is in the middle right away. The men in these positions must learn to backpedal and lead step when covering man and turn sideways and run when playing zone.

The secondary coach can drill on stance by placing his three or four deep in relative positions and hollering "set." Then they pop into their stance. If you have three or four sets of backs, have them all do this at once one behind the other.

### 2. PASS DEFENSE INDIVIDUAL DRILLS

Secondary men use the catch drills described under the linebacker section but should have a greater variety of individual pass defense drills.

### Fight for the Ball Drill

Line up the defenders in pairs and have them face the coach. Have one player from each line run forward as the coach ''lays'' the ball in the air. You can vary this drill by having players line up in the same manner and then having them run backward. Since they are going away from the passer, they will have to adjust to this when they are fighting for the ball.

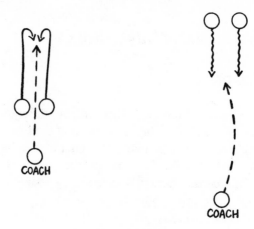

**DIAGRAM #123**

### Falling Down Drill

Many times a pass defender will slip and fall and not recover in time. He may think that because he fell he does not have a chance to make the play. With practice in this drill, defenders learn that they can slip and fall then bounce up and still be in position.

Have the defenders go through their various drills on footwork, covering all types of passes. These drills are to be done by vocal commands from the coach. When the command ''fall'' is given, the defender goes to the ground and quickly recovers and continues the drill. In time your players will hit the ground and bounce right up with surprisingly little loss of time.

### Around the Dummy Drill

Line up your secondary people in a single line facing a passer at about 20 yards. In between, station a standing dummy at ten yards. The first man up runs forward and circles the dummy so that he is now running away from the passer. The passer now throws a variety of passes at the defender. It is most important that the passer throw short, soft, hard, long—anything that makes the defender have to go get the ball.

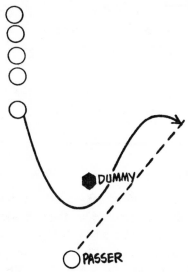

DIAGRAM #124

### Timing Drill

Since the ability to run backward is so important, especially where man-to-man coverage is involved, every pass defender should work on this technique. The trick is to keep the backward stride low—cleats close to the grass. The only incentive for improvement is time. Have every defensive man involved in pass defense run a 15-yard backward sprint. Use a stopwatch and keep records. A very good time is 2.3 seconds.

### Reaction Drill

Station three defensive backs facing the coach. They should be five yards apart to allow space to maneuver. Start the drill by having the players run in place and then give the following five commands: 1) front, 2) back, 3) left, 4) right, and 5) down. When you say "down," have them hit the ground and bounce up, running in place as fast as possible. Insist that all movements be run at right angles. Do not let the players run in an arc. After you have done this for a while, you will notice how much more territory the players can cover between commands.

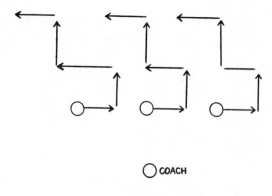

$\bigcirc$ COACH

**DIAGRAM #125**

### Wave Interception Drill

Station a defender on one of the yard lines; the coach faces him with a football at about five yards. Have the defender retreat from the coach, along the yard line. The coach uses the football to point in different directions. The defender turns and runs in the direction indicated. The coach keeps waving the ball so that even though the defender is zig-zagging, he is generally running down the chalk line. After a number of turns, the coach throws the ball where the defender must go and get a difficult reception. You can add to this drill by running two receivers downfield parallel to the defensive back at about eight yards apart. Have the passer throw to one of the receivers. The defender breaks on the ball for the interception. Gradually the distance between the receivers can be increased.

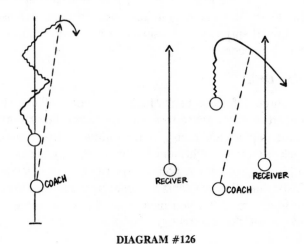

**DIAGRAM #126**

### Break on the Ball Drill

Station two junior varsity receivers downfield to act as stationary targets. At first they should only be about ten yards apart. Station a defensive secondary man between the two stationary targets. The defensive man runs in place while the passer sets up at 15 yards from the targets. The passer fakes, then throws to one of the stationary receivers. The defender reads the passer and breaks for the interception in front of the stationary target. Gradually increase the distance the targets are apart to 18 yards. Also, back the passer up to 20 or 25 yards. In zone coverage, a deep secondary defender should be able to lap nine yards in either direction. This means the three deep can cover the field. This drill can be added to by having the defender line up at eight yards from the passer. On the starting signal, the passer retreats seven yards and sets up to throw to the same stationary targets. The defender retreats about ten yards, still between the targets, and pulls up ready to break on the ball.

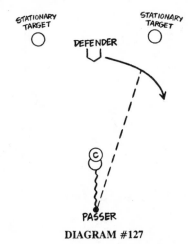

DIAGRAM #127

### Individual Zone Drill

Station one defender in the middle of the field. Establish a line of scrimmage 15 yards in front of him. Set up a center, quarterback and two wide receivers. You will need extra receivers. The two receivers line up, one on each hashmark. The quarterback goes on cadence and sets up to pass in the normal manner. The two wide receivers sprint straight down the hashmarks. The passer lays a long pass down to either receiver. On the snap, the defender retreats straight back, keeping his eyes on the passer. As soon as the passer gives the "long arm action'' and points the ball, the defender breaks for the appropriate hash and adjusts his depth for the interception. Be sure the passer throws on both sides of the defender. When retreating, the defender will always have one side facing one hash. Breaking to that side is easier and quicker. When the ball is thrown to the side away from where the defender is facing, he must learn to pivot back to the proper side. This means taking his eyes off the ball momentarily as his back will be turned to the flight of the ball, but this is still the quickest way to get position.

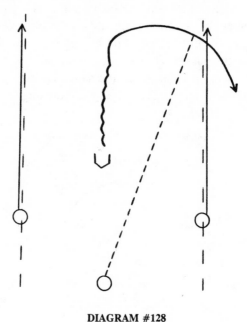

**DIAGRAM #128**

### *Flat Drill*

Set up the passer on one hashmark. His wide receiver is almost to the other hash. In front of the receiver, place a defender. On the starting signal the receiver runs forward five yards and then breaks into the flat area. He also has the optional routes of running directly to the flat or running a flat-and-up. The defender must react first to the quick break. He must not waste extra backward steps in this situation and break up quickly, under control, keeping just enough leverage to cover the route as is or be able to adjust to a cutback. The other two possibilities start out the same. The defender must back straight up until the receiver makes his break to the outside. The defender must not waste backward steps now but must parallel the receiver keeping a reasonable cushion. He should fight for a slight outside leverage. The reason he does not break up on the receiver right away is the possibility of the "up" route. When the ball is thrown to the receiver staying in the flat, the defender has perfect position to break up on the ball playing through the receiver. If the receiver runs a flat-and-up, the defender, who has kept a cushion, can now turn and run with him.

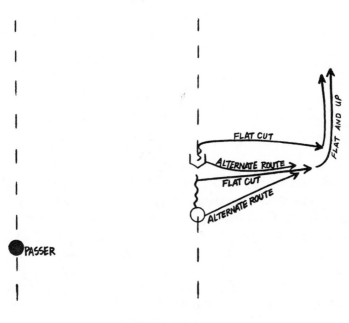

**DIAGRAM #129**

### *Body Position Drill*

Line up all the defensive backs in single file. Use one player to hold a hand shield about six or seven yards from the first player in line, but off to one side. The coach is facing the first man in the single file at 17 or 18 yards' distance. When the coach looks at the player holding the hand shield, the first defender breaks up immediately toward the dummy man. The coach throws the ball directly at the man holding the shield. The defender tries to intercept. As he is intercepting, the man holding the dummy slams the bag into the defender. If the defender does not get body position (turning the side of his body into the bag) during the interception, he will lose control.

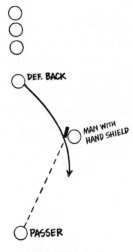

DIAGRAM #130

## Half-Circle Drill

Arrange six players in a half circle. Station one player three yards out in front of the circle. The player in front assumes a defensive stance and moves his feet in place. The coach acts as passer. The player in front must focus his eyes on the coach's eyes. The coach looks at one of the players in the circle and then throws the ball at him. The defender should read the coach's eyes first and then the ball. He should try to align himself between the coach and the player he is looking at before the coach throws the ball. The player who catches the ball returns it to the coach quickly.

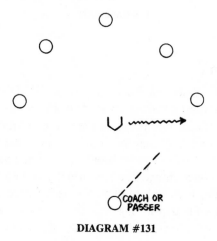

DIAGRAM #131

### Opposite Direction Deflection

Line up in single file the players who are to do the deflecting. They should be located 15 yards from you and should run across the field. Line up the defenders who are to intercept the deflected balls five to eight yards deeper. These players should run, under control, in the opposite direction and will become deflectors in the next line. The passer throws a hard pass to the first line of players. They try to deflect it to the second line of players one at a time.

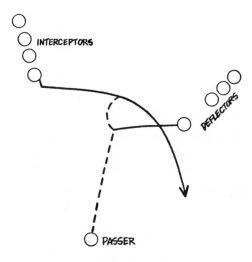

DIAGRAM #132

### Crossing Tip Drill

Form two single lines of pass defenders about ten yards apart facing in the same direction. The passer is downfield facing them at about 20 yards. One line is designated as deflectors and the other as interceptors. The first men in both lines start out together. The man designated as deflector runs ten yards and breaks over the middle. The man designated as interceptor runs five yards and also breaks over the middle but paces himself as he is running less distance. The passer throws the ball high to the deflector who bats it in the air. The interceptor breaks to the deflected ball and intercepts at the highest possible point in its trajectory.

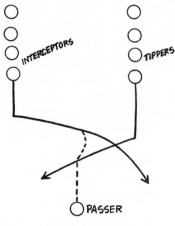

DIAGRAM #133

### Two in One Zone Drill

Use two receivers, center and quarterback on offense. The two receivers are close enough together to release into the same zone. Use one defender positioned as a cornerback or deep halfback and instruct him to play zone. This is the deep one-third of the field on his side. Have one of the two receivers run a deep route and the other a shorter route. This drill teaches the defender to always cover the deepest receiver in the zone first and then break up on the ball if it is thrown to the short man. A good coaching expression to use is "deep as the deepest and wide as the widest." In this drill the defender will find the more width he keeps, the better his position will be to cover both receivers.

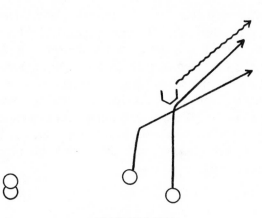

DIAGRAM #134

### Playing the Ball from the Outside Drill

Station a receiver downfield in a position to receive an "out." Locate a defender about five yards behind the receiver and one yard to the outside. The passer is ten yards from the defensive player. Have him throw the ball slightly to the outside of the receiver. The defender tries to intercept or break up the pass. Every so often the passer should throw one directly at the defender, to make sure he is not paying too much attention to the receiver.

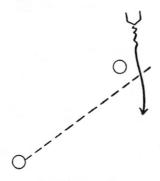

DIAGRAM #135

### Crossing Drill

Use two ends, a center and quarterback on offense. Station a safetyman in his normal position on defense, 10 to 12 yards deep. The two ends run crossing patterns breaking at about six or eight yards. Don't let the passer hold the ball more than four seconds. The safety man gives ground and watches the passer. He should be able to break on the ball and cover the pass, regardless of which end is the receiver.

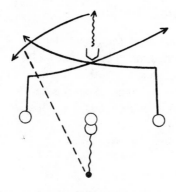

DIAGRAM #136

### Coffin-Corner Interception Drill

Line up the defenders on the goal line in front of the goal-posts. Set the passer on the 45-yard line. Later move him forward to the 40-yard line, then try the 35-yard line. The passer throws a high pass toward either coffin corner. The defender, standing on the goal-line, tries to intercept the ball. If he can't make the catch, he should at least be able to bat the ball down.

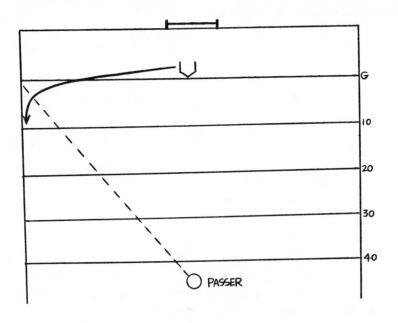

**DIAGRAM #137**

### Jumping Drill

Two defenders stand facing each other as if they were getting ready for the center jump in basketball. The coach stands next to the two players and tosses a football in the air between them. The defenders time their jumps so they reach the ball at its highest point. They must play the ball with both hands. Do not allow them to use a hand on their opponent. They want to develop good habits in jumping so they won't cause a penalty for interference.

DIAGRAM #138

## 3. TACKLING DRILLS

The following tackling drills are described elsewhere in this book but should be used by the secondary people.

- The three-yard open-field tackle drill
- The running blocker drill
- The shuffle and lift, shoulder tackling drill
- The eye-opener linebacker drill
- The back-to-back tackling drill
- The Oklahoma drill

Here are some drills specifically for deep backs:

### Dummy Key and Support Drill

Set up an offensive tight end and full backfield. Align a corner back in his regular position and have him key the tight end and near back. On run key, the cornerback comes up right away and uses a two-hand tag on the ballcarrier. He must turn the run in so you can add to this drill by using a blocker ahead of the ballcarrier. Occasionally, have the tight end release so the corner will have to play pass as well as run.

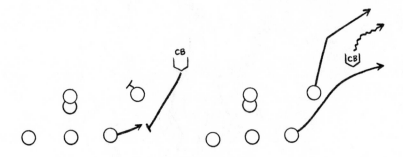

DIAGRAM #139

### *Sweep Tackling Drill*

Put a standing dummy 12 yards from the sideline. Station the defenders in a line just inside the dummy. They should start the drill at eight yards from the dummy. The ballcarriers must run a sweep between the dumm and the sideline. The defenders learn to use the sideline as part of their leverage on the ball. Defenders support quickly to the line of scrimmage then come to collection and shuffle into their tackle. They learn how to hem a back up against the sideline when he is without a lead blocker. This requires a slight inside-out approach. When you add a blocker to this drill, the defender must keep outside leverage on the blocker.

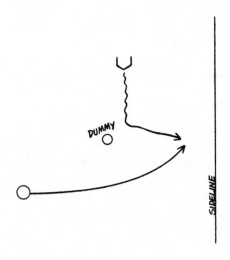

DIAGRAM #140

### Goal-Line Tackling Drill

Get a line of ballcarriers ready to go one at a time. Facing them are the defensive backs who come up one at a time also. The ballcarriers are on the five-yard line and the defenders are on the two-yard line. On the starting signal, the ballcarriers must run at an outside or inside angle and they must try to cross the goal line. The defenders tackle to prevent the score.

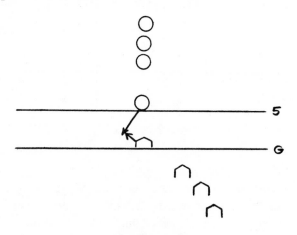

DIAGRAM #141

### Sideline Tackling Drill

Use a line of reserve backs as ballcarriers. The coach throws the football to the first back in line as he runs straight upfield along the sideline. The defender stalks the ballcarrier and tries to get his head in front when making the tackle. He may have to knock him out of bounds or even push him out of bounds if he fails in getting good position. The players will note the difference in yards gained.

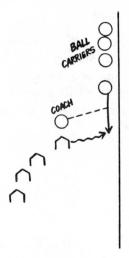

**DIAGRAM #142**

### On-Balance Drill

The ballcarrier and defender start out 12 yards apart. On the starting signal, they sprint towards each other. When the defender gets into tackling range, he slows down and gets a good base. Allow the ballcarrier only two fakes. The tackler shuffles into the tackle. Don't let the tacklers go for low tackles in the open field.

**DIAGRAM #143**

# 5

# DEFENSIVE SEMI-GROUP, GROUP, AND TEAM DRILLS

## A. SEMI-GROUP DRILLS

### 1. TRAP AND POWER DRILL

This drill features two defensive linemen who play alongside each other. The idea is to teach them to play the trap. Straight blocking and wedges should be mixed in to keep the two defensemen honest, but basically you are teaching reaction to traps. The exact setup depends on the type of defensive front used by your team. The three-on-two is needed if your scheme is some form of six-man front. All the other defenses need a four-on-two. For example, suppose you use a 4-3 defense. You will need a center, two guards and one tackle on offense against a defensive tackle and end. The defensive end lines up on the offensive tackle and the defensive tackle lines up on the offensive guard. From this setup the offensive blockers run some straight blocking but mostly traps on the defensive end and defensive tackle. This is a full-speed drill and presents the defenders with blocking patterns they must meet. If the trap is on the defensive end, the defensive tackle must fight the double team and the end of the trap. If the trap is on the tackle, he must read this and react and the end fights the cutoff and must take a pursuit angle. There should be an offensive huddle before each play.

If your defensive scheme is some form of odd line, the middle guard lines up on the center and his teammate is now either an eagle tackle or a 5-4 tackle. The same plays are run at these two defenders from the same four offensive linemen.

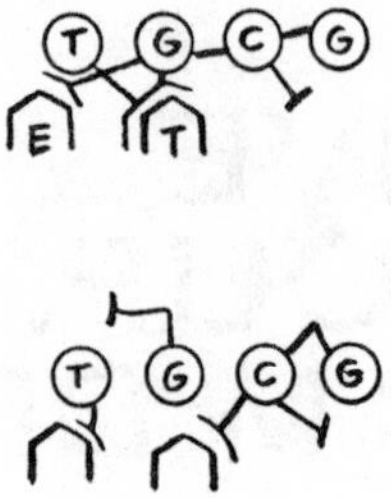

DIAGRAM #144

## 2. FIVE-ON-TWO DRILL

Using the same idea as the preceding drill, you now line up five offensive blockers (center, two guards and two tackles) against two defensive linemen aligned in an even defense. From this setup, using a huddle every play, the entire offensive blocking patterns that affect the middle can be run.

DIAGRAM #145

### 3. FIVE-ON-THREE DRILL

Add a middle linebacker to the preceding drill. This allows for the interaction of the middle of the defense. You are producing a full-speed key-reading drill. All three defenders work on their middle techniques. Stunts can be used, but they should be used sparingly. Blitzes and stunts should be practiced against dummies or "posts" to achieve timing but the majority of time should be spent on reaction defenses. You must perfect your base defense. If you can't play that, all the stunts in the world won't help you.

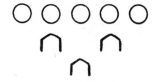

DIAGRAM #146

### 4. OUTSIDE LINEBACKER AND END DRILL

On the 4-3 defense, the ends and outside linebackers must work together a lot. On the tight end side, the drill is sometimes called the triangle drill. Offensively you use a tight end, tackle, and near back. They run reach blocks, turnout blocks, cross-blocks and double team with the near-back kickout block. The very first place you start to build a defense is right here at the off-tackle hole. If your end and strong linebacker can't close the off-tackle hole, look out, you're in trouble.

The split end side presents a different picture. The weak linebacker and end must continually use inside and outside techniques. These are not stunts but just a switching of whole responsibility. Also, your weak linebacker must learn to play against a tight end on his side.

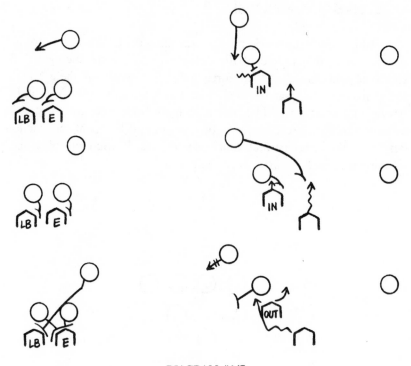

DIAGRAM #147

## 5. PASS-RUSH DRILL

Within semi-groups, it is advisable to work on pass rush, draw and screen. The idea is to concentrate on any of the preceding semi-groups with nothing but keys that show pass. It is not too good to combine the pass situation. It should be worked on separately. In small groups such as these, the important things such as technique, rushing lanes, etc., can be observed much easier. It almost takes a separate drill to teach ends to read screen. This drill features pass show with pass blocking, pass show with draw blocking and pass show with screen blocking. The first time your opponents run a screen at you, and your end smells the phony block and breaks off his contain rush and shuffles out into the middle of the screen, you'll be glad you spent some time on this drill.

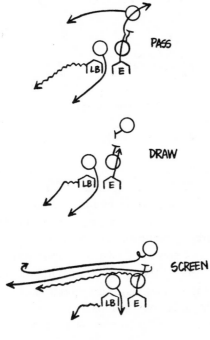

DIAGRAM #148

## 6. UP AND DOWN THE LINE READING DRILL

In a 4-3 setup, place all four down linemen in their normal positions against a full offensive line. The coach starts out behind the strong end and by use of hand signals, directs all the situations that will ever come up against that one end. He must read and react to reach, turn out, cross, trap, pass, double team and near back lead. These are done quickly. As soon as one block has been executed, the end lines back up, the signal is given and a quick "hike" is used. After he finishes with the strong end, the coach moves quickly behind the strong tackle and repeats the procedure. This is done until all four linemen have read and reacted to every situation. This takes a bit more time than you'd like, but every day every lineman must read full-speed keys.

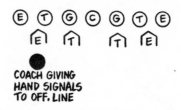

COACH GIVING
HAND SIGNALS
TO OFF. LINE

DIAGRAM #149

## 7. SAM AND MIKE PASS DRILL

The strong linebacker and the middle linebacker in a 4-3 defense are required to play the second and third eligibles on pass plays. On other types of defenses the positions may change, but the idea here is that wherever two linebackers or a linebacker and safety must play a combination coverage, there should be a drill to train them. This particular drill should show the two linebackers at which point they play man and which point they play combination zone. Distance apart is the key. When the second and third eligible pass receivers align so that they are seven yards apart or closer, the two defenders must play an inside-outside zone. This is to prevent crosses and picks. When the two eligibles are more than seven yards apart, the strong safety gets involved. Also, when Sam is on the blitz, then Mike must cover the #3 man and vice-versa. All these situations must be covered.

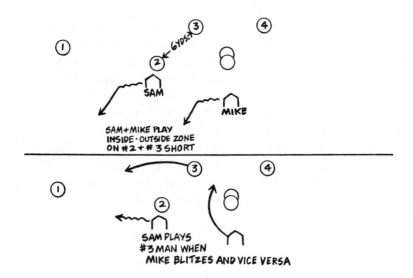

DIAGRAM #150

## 8. WILL AND WEAK SAFETY PASS DRILL

In a 4-3, both Will (weak linebacker) and the weak safety key the #4 eligible. This is the fourth eligible counting from the strong side. When #4 declares weak, the weak safety can support weak. Will knows he can play #4 tougher and get help deep. If #4 declares strong, then the weak safety must support strong. Will now must get position to fill the void between the weak safety and weak corner. Now these may not be your particular pass rules, but drills like this must be used to show the interplay between the positions.

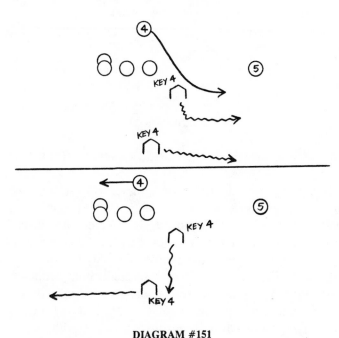

DIAGRAM #151

## 9. CORNER AND STRONG SAFETY PASS DRILL

Using the same format as outlined in the preceding drills, the corners and safeties must be drilled in man and combination coverages.

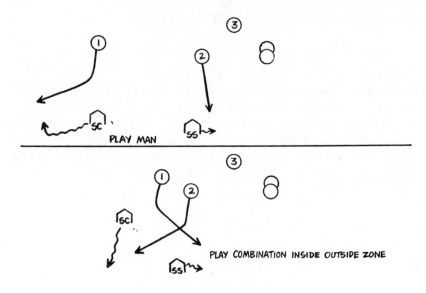

DIAGRAM #152

## 10. THREE LINEBACKER ZONE POSITION DRILL

All you need for this drill is one quarterback and a marked field. Position the quarterback on the hashmark. Against him line up three linebackers in the proper alignment. If your defense calls for two linebackers and two ends, or two linebackers and one end, or whatever, you are working with the people who play the short zones in a zone defense. The quarterback goes through three actions one at a time. He rolls to the wide side, rolls to the weak side and drops straight back. The defenders work on rotation to the field and rotation to the boundary. The whole drill is position: position with regard to the rotation, position with regard to the field, and position with regard to the ball. The first time you do this, you'll find defenders slap up against the boundary and a wide variance as to distance apart. It's easy to draw up four short zones across the field, but there is a lot more to it than that.

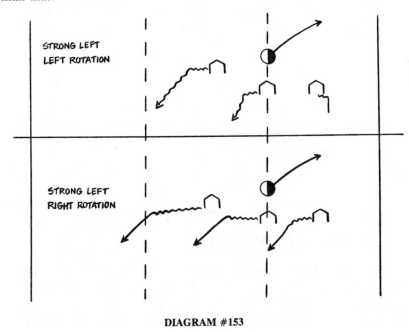

STRONG LEFT
LEFT ROTATION

STRONG LEFT
RIGHT ROTATION

**DIAGRAM #153**

## 11. FOUR DEEP ZONE POSITION DRILL

Use the same format as the short zone position drill. It will help to set up a flanker, tight end and split end so strength may be declared.

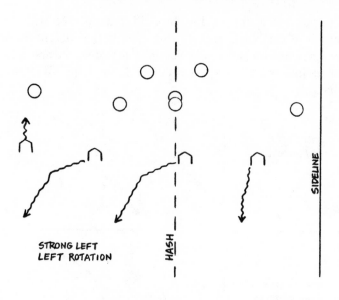

**DIAGRAM #154**

## 12. DOUBLE-COVER DRILL

Set up a center, quarterback and one wide receiver. Against the wide receiver, employ two defenders who must cover him short and deep. There are many ways to do this and it is done by a variety of positions. The first way to practice this maneuver is to rotate into the wide receiver. Another way is to pre-declare, and the same two positions are usually involved. Either way, the defender assigned to cover the receiver short can get right on his nose and "dog" him tight for ten yards; or he can fake getting on him and then back up five yards and zone him; or he might surprise him with collision and recovery. No matter what the method, the short man must take away the ten-yard pass play. When he loses him, the deep man picks him up and prevents the long gainer.

Another double-cover drill involves the weak linebacker who must use the same procedures. It is useful to work on game situations with the double-cover drill. Late in the half or game, the time-out situation is important. If the offensive opponent is short of time-outs remaining, he must go to the sideline. This means the short double-cover man must align outside the wide receiver and force him into the field. If the offense has all their time-outs, the double cover man should approach the receiver from the inside taking away the middle cuts.

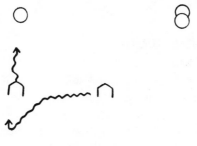

**DIAGRAM #155**

## 13. BUMP-AND-RUN DRILL

This drill is included in semi-groups because, except for the very talented athlete, the bump-and-runner should be backed up deep. It is a form of double-cover. However, you might try this drill to see if you have a corner who can use this style of pass defense on occasion. Get your two or three fastest receivers and line them up one at a time and have your corner align on the first up at eight yards. You need a center, quarterback, and a cadence. Just before the center passes to the quarterback, the corner sneaks up on the receiver's inside shoulder, taking all the line of scrimmage he can get without being offsides. The defender's outside foot is back and he actually cannot see the quarterback. On the first movement by the receiver, the defender attacks him with a shoulder and flipper, forcing the receiver to the outside. When the receiver begins to slip by, the defender must turn and run with him. At no time does the defender take his eyes off the receiver. He must notice when the receiver looks back for the ball and prepares to receive. At this point the defender must also locate the ball and play it. This maneuver should not be attempted unless there is a pressing defense up front. The rushers can't let the receiver get too far down field. They must make the quarterback throw. A general rule is zone-reading defenses and press man-to-man coverages.

**DIAGRAM #156**

# B. GROUP DRILLS

### 1. HALF-LINE SCRIMMAGE

Use the same setup described under the offensive drills in this book for half-line scrimmage except the emphasis is now on defense. On one side of the field, use a center, the strong guard, tackle and tight end with a full backfield. Against them use a defensive tackle and end with a strong linebacker, middle linebacker and the strong corner and strong safety. The offense runs their strong side offense both run and pass. You will want to use only those passes that involve the strong side such as play action and sprints. Do not run straight drops.

On the other side of the field use the weak side personnel on both offense and defense. When you scrimmage this way you can get a great deal more done than in full scrimmage because there is no "off" side.

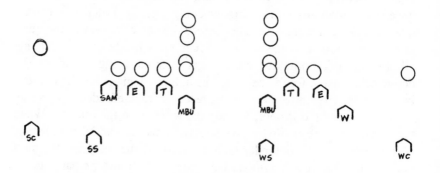

DIAGRAM #157

### 2. FRONT-SEVEN STUNTS DRILL

Earlier, the training aid called the offensive posts was described. Six large posts are placed in the ground and are spaced as offensive linemen. Old shoulder pads and headgear are put on top to further simulate offensive players. During the season, the appropriate colored jerseys are pulled over the pads so that each week a little more realism is added. Place a football on the ground in front of the third post in on either side to establish the center. This leaves three posts on one side of the center and two on the other. Naturally, the three-post side is the strong side and the two-post side is the weak or split end side. Take your first two varsity defensive units, minus the secondary, and align them in front of the posts. The first unit lines up in position first and the second unit lines up five yards behind their own positions. The coach calls the defense and the ''hike.'' Quickly the unit executes their defensive assignment and hustles out of the way. The second unit steps forward and the same procedure is repeated. You can go through the whole defensive repertoire in a relatively short period of time. This is an excellent way to rehearse all the stunts.

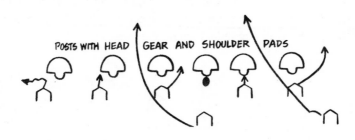

POSTS WITH HEAD  GEAR  AND  SHOULDER  PADS

**DIAGRAM #158**

## 3. ROTATION DRILL

The four deep backs need separate work on rotations. First they must learn reaction to the flow of the ball when not in a zone. Next they must rotate to assignments when a zone is called and then react to the ball. The basic way to start teaching this is to use just one quarterback with the ball. Call the defense and let the ballcarrier go right, left and back. Use a whistle any time during the movement to cause the defense to freeze. You can check their relationship to each other and the boundary. Occasionally have the quarterback reverse his field; again whistle the action dead and check the position of the secondary.

## 4. FOUR-DEEP RECOGNITION DRILL

The secondary must recognize offensive sets. Everyone may have a different system for doing this, but whatever the system, the three or four deep people need a lot of looking at different formations and making their calls. The drill doesn't involve any action on the part of the offense other than lining up. The offense needs a full backfield and two ends with one center. After each huddle, the offense quickly lines up and the defensive four deep make their calls and line up. That's all there is to it. Offense huddles again and the process is repeated. The coach must prepare a ''script'' of offensive formations so everything can be covered.

Here is an example of how this drill works. Defense called is man-for-man with one free safety. The offense comes out of the huddle and lines up strong right. Defensive safeties call ''strong left.'' Safeties then align accordingly. Safeties then make a call for man or combination zone to their corners depending on the width of the receivers. If a zone had been called, the direction of the rotation is repeated by all four secondary men.

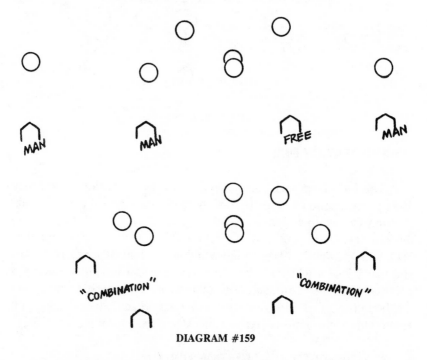

DIAGRAM #159

## 5. FOUR-DEEP VS. PATTERNS DRILL

Use the same setup as the preceding drill. Now you add routes. Concentrate on certain types of routes such as crossing patterns, hooks and curls, post, look-in, etc. You may start out by walking through the routes and coverages, especially early in the season.

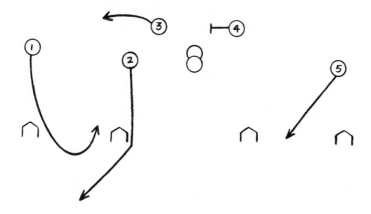

DIAGRAM #160

## 6. ONE-HALF PERIMETER DRILL

One of the toughest positions to play is strong linebacker. He is part of the pass defense on drop-back passes and a container on sprint-out passes. The rest of the secondary must play sprints differently from straight drops. This drill works on the tough decisions.

Offensively you need a center, quarterback, near halfback, tight end and flanker. Defensively you need a strong linebacker, strong corner and two safeties. The offense runs drop-back passes, pull-up passes and sprintout passes. On drop-back and pull-up passes, the strong linebacker shuffles out, gaining width, and then gains depth so he can play inside-outside zone with Mike. Against sprintouts, the strong linebacker shuffles out first and then when he realizes he's facing a full sprint, comes upfield to contain. A strong linebacker axiom is "when in doubt, shuffle out." Also, the twin safeties must shift gears when playing a full sprint. Normally the strong safety backs up Sam and Mike deep and the weak safety is free—free in a sense that he keys #4. If there is a full sprint, #4 will have to come strong to block, if the offense wants to release #3 in the strong pattern. This means the twin safeties now play inside-outside on #2 and #3. The weak safety can do this because #4 brought him strong. If #4 didn't come strong but there is a full sprint strong, then #3 will have to block and the strong safety will have to cover #2 man-for-man. All of this is necessary because Sam must contain a full sprint.

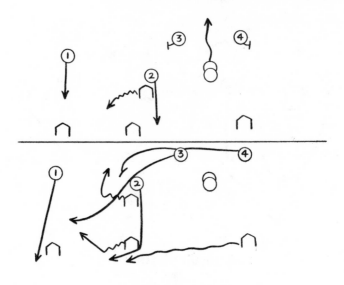

**DIAGRAM #161**

## 7. LAPPING DRILL

This is a zone drill. Use the four deep against a passer. Call the rotation. The quarterback takes the snap and sets up. The four deep rotates to a three deep. The passer throws between the defenders. The logical interceptor calls for the ball and the next closest defender backs him up. Be sure to work on a marked field so that halfbacks can "lap" with the sideline.

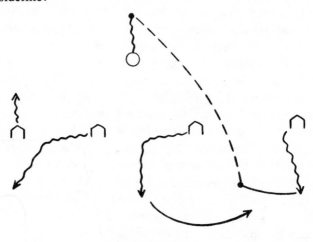

**DIAGRAM #162**

## 8. ZONE CONFIDENCE DRILL

Use a full offensive team against the pass defense perimeter of seven defenders. Call a zone defense. Make all ten men on the offense eligible to receive a pass. On the snap the defense rotates (or aligns) to zone position. The passer tries to pass to any one of ten receivers. If all the defensemen have proper position in their zone, they will be able to break up the pass. Make the passer throw within four seconds.

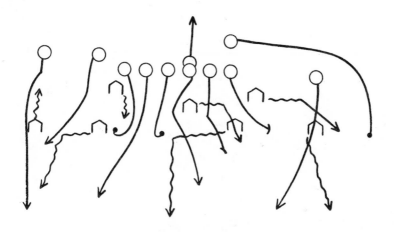

DIAGRAM #163

## 9. FULL-PERIMETER DRILL

This drill can get more done than any other drill for defense. It utilizes time and personnel the best. Two basic defensive units work at the same time at opposite ends of the playing field. One group is the perimeter people and the other is basically a line group. The linebackers swing. The perimeter group works off the far 40-yard line. The line group works from the 20 to the goal line. The perimeter has all the four deep, plus one set of linebackers. They work against an offensive setup of a full backfield and two ends. (You will need spare offensive receivers.) The line group has all the down-linemen plus one set of linebackers. They work against a full offense minus wide receivers. The perimeter gets mostly all passes with an occasional draw and sweep. The line group works mostly against the run with an occasional draw or short pass. Halfway through the drill, the linebackers swap. This drill is a *must*. At least 40 minutes a day should be spent on this.

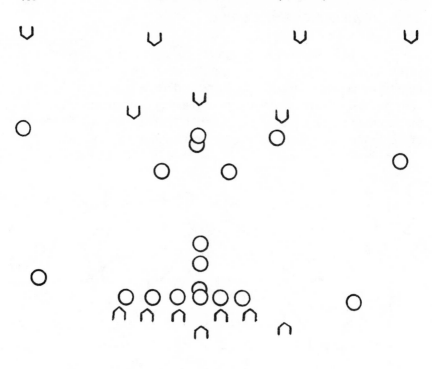

DIAGRAM #164

## 10. GREEN BAY DRILL

This is a full-speed drill. Line up the regular four deep backs in their normal positions. Place four offensive receivers between or outside the defenders in any fashion. Have a passer throw a pass that is high and long and easy to intercept. As soon as one of the defenders intercepts the ball, his "team" becomes the offense and the receivers now become the defense. The interceptor's team blocks and the other group tries to tackle the ballcarrier. Linebackers can be used in this drill. This drill requires 40 yards of the field. It is a good drill early in the season when you are trying to find out about rookies and tryouts. The aggressive defenders will show up.

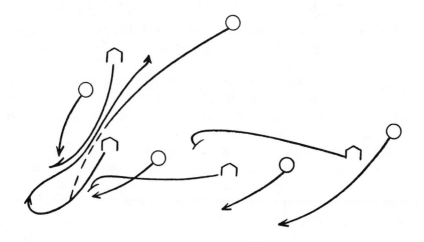

DIAGRAM #165

## C. DEFENSIVE TEAM DRILLS

### 1. PURSUIT DRILL

Take one full unit of 11 defensive players and line them up in front of seven offensive linemen. Put the seven offensive linemen on their hands and knees with head held high. (You can also use the seven-man sled for this drill.) The ball should be in the exact middle of the field. Behind the center is a single line of running backs. Station two standing dummies five yards inside each sideline on the line of scrimmage. On the starting signal, the running back with the ball sprints towards either standing dummy. The defensive front makes a one-step charge into the passive offensive player and then reacts laterally to the flow of the ball. The defensive corner on the side of flow comes up fast and makes a two-handed tag on the ballcarrier. He is the first to tag. The middle (or inside) linebacker makes the next tag behind the line of scrimmage. Inside linebackers always approach wide plays from inside out. The next tag is from the inside safety who comes up quickly but levels off at the line of scrimmage and always supports or backs up his corner. If there is a wide flanker set out, then the inside safety becomes the force and makes the first tag. The ball-carrier keeps running for the dummy and turns upfield between the dummy and the sideline. The defensive outside linebacker, or 5-4 end, makes the tag on the ballcarrier right after he rounds the bag. Next, in order, the defensive end and two tackles make their tags at about four-yard intervals. The offside end is chase man and trails the ballcarrier one yard deeper than the carrier's path. The next tag is made by the off-safety. He is followed by the off-side outside linebacker and last by the off-side corner who makes the last tag. When the speed of the ballcarrier is swift and constant, the angles of pursuit will bring the defensive player to the proper spot of contact.

This drill can be varied by having the ballcarrier start wide and cut back at any point in his run. It will be easy to see if any defensive player has failed to keep leverage on the ball.

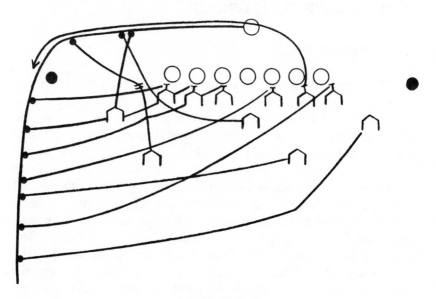

DIAGRAM #166

## 2. INTERCEPTION DRILL

Take a center and quarterback on offense and line up a full defense in front of them. The quarterback takes and sets up to pass at seven yards. Defensive rushers and containers "cup" the passer. The defensive backs and linebackers get to their zones and square up. The passer throws a high lob anywhere. The interceptor calls for the ball, the proper defender backs him up, and the rest of the defense now switches to offense and sprints for position ahead of the ball. After a good 30-yard sprint, all blockers do a forward shoulder roll.

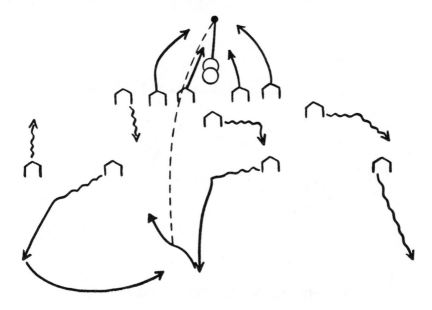

DIAGRAM #167

## 3. DEFENSIVE TEAM DUMMY DRILL

There are times when your defense cannot afford to hit. Such times are usually just before the game and the first practice after the game. It takes a well-disciplined scouting team to put on a well-timed play without much contact. They must learn to just stick out a shoulder and let the defense react. Running blockers learn to become passive at the contact point. Ballcarriers give up if there is no passable route. The hardest thing to stop is the defensive position which does not allow ballcarrier progress. Yet, if you are going to check pursuit angles, the ballcarrier must be allowed to run out the play.

You need one full offensive team with spares in the positions that run a lot, such as backs and wide receivers. It would be nice to have two full offensive teams run plays at your defense, but few teams have enough personnel for this. Be sure you move the ball from hash to hash and up and down the field.

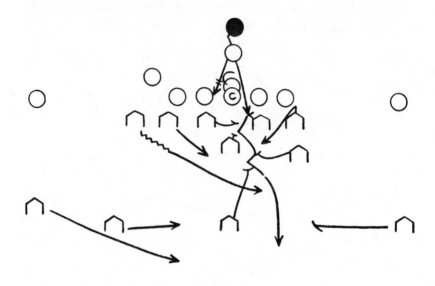

**DIAGRAM #168**

## 4. DEFENSIVE TEAM FULL-SPEED DUMMY DRILL

This is the same drill as the preceding one, but it is a lot more realistic. It should be done in full gear on work days. The only thing that is different from full scrimmage is that you eliminate tackling. This prevents pileups and reduces the possibility of injury. Defensive players get in position to tackle but allow the ballcarrier to run out the play. This is not as easy to get done as it sounds. It isn't natural to "pull up" after defeating a blocker. Also, in spite of the coaches' instructions, the offense feels they are supposed to get beat and will "dog it" if allowed to. A scout-team coach with a sense of drive and a sense of humor is a great asset in this drill. It is a good idea to use this drill up and down the field, but when you come to the goal-line area, tell both offense and defense the rules are off. Go full tilt and tell the scout team to score if they can. Only hit about four plays this way and then turn around and go back to full-speed dummy. This brief scrimmage will pick up both teams.

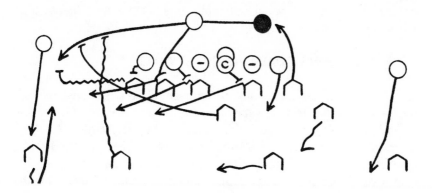

DIAGRAM #169

## 5. DEFENSIVE TEAM SITUATIONS SCRIMMAGE

This is scrimmage all the way but you want to concentrate on situations. Areas of the field, down and distance, and time remaining are all types of situations you can work on. Most teams work longer on third-down situations than any other. It is a good drill for both offense and defense and is one of the times you will want to go with your number-one offense against your number-one defense. This is because third-down-and-long will result in a lot of passing and both offensive receivers and defensive pass defenders need work against swifter people. There is no diagram necessary for this drill.

## 6. DEFENSIVE TEAM WATCH DRILL

After giving your defensive team the opponent's offensive scouting report on Monday in the meeting room, it is a good idea to go over it again on the field. Simply have the scout team run the offense at your defense who just watches from their normal alignment. The idea is to show the whole team just what the opponent's overall scheme is trying to do. List the things you must stop in order of importance. Tell your team that you are going to take away what your opponent does best. It is important that you keep the "stop" list fairly small. There are only about seven or eight outstanding things that any offensive team can do. This is also a good time to cover tendencies. Place the ball on a hash and run what your opponent's tendencies are off this particular hash. All the defense does is watch and think. It is much more effective than a blackboard report.

## 7. DEFENSIVE GOAL-LINE RALLY DRILL

This is full-speed goal-line scrimmage. Give the offense the ball on the five-yard line with four downs in which to score. Get all the offensive players on the squad and line them up ten yards behind the offensive huddle. Also get all the defensive players (frosh, B-team, managers, everybody) and line them up on the end zone back line. The offensive bunch roots, cheers and hollers for the offense, and the defensive crowd does the same for the defense. The more noise the better. If the band is practicing nearby, get them in action for a while. Both units must get used to the fact that nothing stimulates crowd noise like the close goal-line situation. You don't need to do this long, and it is a great way to wind up practice.

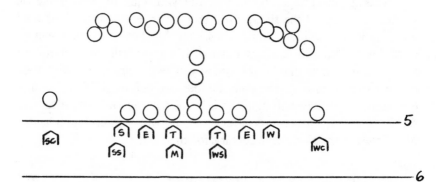

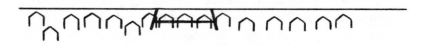

**DIAGRAM #170**

# 6
# KICKING DRILLS

## A. PUNTING DRILLS

### 1. STANCE AND STEPS DRILL

The first job is to set the stance, to discover how the feet should be placed at the beginning of a kick. Before making any kind of punt, the kicker should stand with the kicking foot forward. Thus, most kickers will find they need take but one step with the non-kicking foot before they kick with the other. This eliminates the unnecessary extra step most untrained kickers take.

Have the kicker take his stance until he feels both comfortable and solidly set and while in this position, push him forward, back, left and right. If his feet are poorly placed, the kicker will easily be pushed off balance. Balance is an integral part of each good, accurate kick.

After the kicker has found his correct stance, have him practice making his kicking steps and go through the motions of kicking the football. No ball is needed in this drill for steps. He is just trying to get the "feel" of the act.

Sometimes it helps to outline the position of the feet throughout the kicking procedure. Chalk marks or dye can be placed on the grass. In this way the kicker can check himself as he practices the dry-run kick. Soon the footwork will become second nature.

### 2. FOOT-POSITION DRILL

This is more of an exercise. Everyone cannot point his foot to full extension at first. Kickers should practice pointing their toes daily. This means really bringing the heel up and the toes down. During warmup, the kicker should sit on the ground and have a teammate (or manager) grab his toes and depress them keeping the heel solidly on the ground. He should also take 10 to 15 short jab steps each day stressing the pointing of the toe.

### 3. KICKING WITHOUT CENTER SNAP DRILL

Punters will want to practice kicking many times when a center is not available. They should get several balls together at one place. They want to simulate the ball striking the hands. An important part of the kicking performance is the quick manipulation of the ball in the hands. This is necessary to get the laces up and to extend the ball forward, ready to place it on the foot.

An excellent drill for this is done by tossing the ball a few inches into the air, quickly adjusting it the moment it strikes the hands, then going through all the motions of kicking the football.

After the kicker has kicked all the balls, he goes to the other end of the field and shags the balls so he can kick them back.

### 4. DROP DRILL

Faulty punting usually results from a poor drop from the hands to the moving foot. Have the punters go through the kicking procedure but don't let them kick the ball. Check the drop. Another way to do this is to just "bunt" the ball. Kickers will quickly see a good drop and rhythmical leg swing will get unusual distance without much force.

### 5. FOOT AND BALL RELATIONSHIP DRILL

Have the kicker mark the middle seam on the underside of the ball with soft white chalk before he kicks the ball. After the kicker has completed his follow-through, observe the line made by the chalked middle seam on the instep. If that line is at a slight angle to the inside of the kicking shoe and crosses the laces about midway, then you should have a good punt.

## 6. FORM AND ACCURACY DRILL

Distance is not a concern in this drill. Make sure the kicker understands that. This is a short kicking drill at a set target.

Have the kicker work with another player about ten yards apart. The kicker just meets the ball and practices until he gets it to the other man. The receiving player should hold his hands up as a target. The kicker should always check his stance, see that his running foot and the nose of the ball are pointed in the direction of the target. Always see that the ball is held properly.

This is a good time to practice raising or lowering the point on the drop to gain loft or kick a line drive. Gradually lengthen the distance in this drill.

## 7. RHYTHM AND SPEED DRILL

The action of the kicker can be timed quite accurately by a stopwatch. First, clock the time from when the center passes to when the ball reaches the kicker's hands. Next, time the speed with which the kicker kicks the ball after it has reached his hands. Third, time the whole process. In this manner you can determine just when the kicking action is being delayed. The common causes of delay are:

1. Center snap is slow or arches like a rainbow;
2. The kicker didn't move into the ball when receiving it;
3. The kicker fiddles with the ball too much getting it set for the drop;
4. The kicker takes too many steps.

Be sure you time this from the exact distance your kicking formation dictates. If you punt from the spread punt, the kicker should align at 14 yards.

## 8. PUNT UNDER PRESSURE DRILL

This is a good drill for center, punter and defensemen who are logical punt blockers. Place the rushers on either side of the center out about seven yards. Allow only one rusher from either side to come on the snap and try to block the kick. The kicker kicks without any blocking. If the kicker is back 14 yards, the center snap is perfect, and the kicker kicks quickly and on rhythm, the blocker will have to get a real jump on the snap to block the kick. This forces kicker concentration. It also makes the center realize his importance in the kicking game. Further, the rushers learn to go for the ball out in front of the kicker. There is nothing more frustrating than to finally get your opponent stopped, force him to punt and then have one of your defenders rough the kicker.

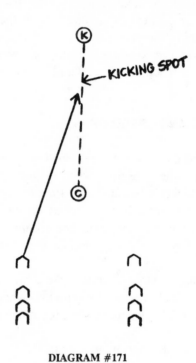

DIAGRAM #171

## 9. PUNTER CONCENTRATION DRILL

Have two centers side by side. The first center is the real center and snaps first. After the punter receives the ball, have the other center rifle another ball at the kicker. The second ball may cause the kicker to lose balance or draw his eyes off the ball he is supposed to kick, or both.

Suddenly cross in front of the kicker while he is about to kick.

Get up a crowd around the kicker with only a narrow opening to kick through. Have them shout and try other distractions.

Once in a while center back a wet ball without the kicker's knowledge.

Some of these things will at first bother the kicker, but they can be applied to benefit him tremendously.

## 10. BAD-PASS DRILL

Take the offensive team to their own one-yard line and declare fourth down. The kicker is now lined up on the restraining line. Go through the kicking procedure, but do not allow defenders to block the kick if they break through the protection. The center purposely snaps bad passes. They are high, low and to either side. The passes are receivable but just off enough to cause problems.

Another bad-pass drill involves just the kicker and a coach. Use this as a pre-game warmup drill. The coach rolls back bouncing balls to the kicker who must field the ball and get the kick away. You must always drill for the unexpected.

## 11. TEAM PUNTING DRILL

Use a full offensive team in a kicking situation. Against them have seven or eight rushers and one safetyman. Make the punt rush full-speed and the punt coverage full-speed up to the tackling point. The idea is to protect the kick and cover the kick but reduce the injury possibility that would exist if you allowed full-speed punt returns. The covering team can more easily be checked to see if they are in lanes without defensive blockers in the way. Also, the covering team must come to collection as they move in for the tackle. Station a coach down by the punt receiver to call the coverage to collection as they near the ball.

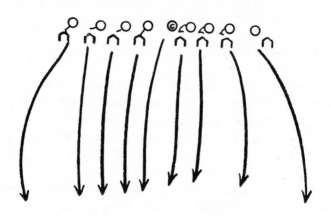

COACH

S

DIAGRAM #172

## B. PUNT RECEIVING DRILLS

Every time the punters are punting, the punt return men should receive. They should work mostly around the ten-yard line, and there should be a coach with them to correct mistakes. The following points are checked: get under the ball; don't try to field a ball you are not "under"; catch the ball in the hands and then bring the ball into the body; when the ball hits the hands, the elbows and knees give a little with the drop of the ball; put the ball away and start to run.

### 1. FAIR-CATCH DRILL

Always have a time for practice in fielding fair catches. The procedure is the same as catching punts for return except that when the ball reaches the receiver's hands and the elbows and knees give, go right to the ground with the left knee. This leaves the right knee directly under the "basket" made by the hands and arms. This prevents the ball from slipping through and reduces the fumble possibility.

### 2. TEAM PUNT RETURN DRILL

The scout team punts to the defense. The rush may be full-speed and the blocking pattern is sprinted to, but knock off the contact at that point. A good way to keep this realistic is to have the blockers grab the covering team in both arms as a signal to stop. Be sure and kick from both hashmarks as well as from the middle of the field.

Every punt return has points that must be followed:

1. There must be someone to force the kicker to kick. Usually the offside rush will force the kicker to kick the ball to the side you wish to return.
2. Occupy as many kick covers as you can for as long as you can.
3. Form a blocking wall that is equally spaced from receiver to line of scrimmage.
4. The three deep men should be placed to receive short or squibbed kicks but still be in the blocking pattern.
5. One deep man always insures the catch by being a personal guard against the first man down.
6. On sideline returns, the returner should always head upfield first to draw in the coverage.
7. There should always be a man in the wall assigned to check the area between the wall and the sideline for "lurkers."

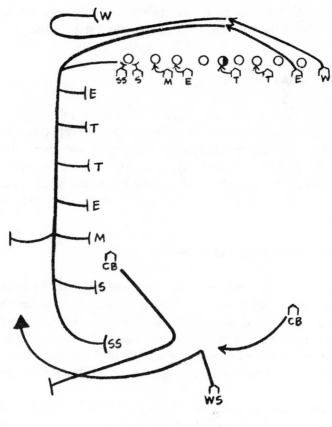

DIAGRAM #173

## 3. TEAM PUNT RETURN DRILL AGAINST THE WIND

In order to save time and avoid confusion, set up a kicking team in position to punt. Alternate the two defensive units against this setup. When the ball is snapped, the offense remains passive and does not cover. The defense goes through their assignments of rush and delay and forms the downfield pattern. The punt receiver catches and runs the play out. The next team jumps in and executes the return.

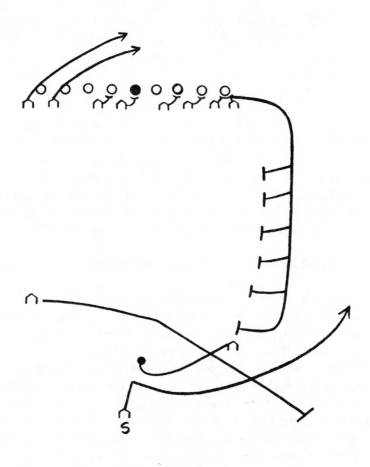

**DIAGRAM #174**

# C. PLACE-KICKING DRILLS

## 1. INDIVIDUAL KICKING POSITION DRILL

In place kicking, the kicker is approaching a fixed object: the ball. The kicker must have his steps down so pat that every time he makes an approach, his feet will fall in exactly the same pattern and have precisely the same spacing. He can't expect to accomplish this by guesswork. He must mark his steps.

To mark his steps, stand with the kicking foot as it would contact the ball when the kick is made. Put a marker (piece of canvas or white cardboard) under the non-kicking foot. Then take a long step backwards to measure the distance covered by the forward hop. Bring the feet together so that the marker may be put underneath the kicking foot. Take another, but shorter, step backward with the non-kicking foot. Next bring the kicking foot alongside it and the kicker should be in starting position. The kicker is now ready to kick.

## 2. PLACE-KICKING CONTACT-POINT DRILL

In practice the ball should be marked with an inverted pyramid centered on the seam in the lower half of the ball. The bottom point is placed on the rear middle seam, just three inches up from the bottom end of the ball. The top line is three inches higher (six inches up from the bottom end of the ball) and is three inches long. It is drawn at right angles to the middle seam, extending out one and one half inches on each side of it. Mark it with dark-colored chalk. Mark a white dot on the front of the kicking toe. The white dot will show up on the ball when it is kicked. After each kick, note carefully just where the foot hit the ball. Having determined this, wipe the area *within* the triangle clean for the next kick. Be sure not to erase the triangle or the line on the rear seam of the ball because they may give additional information as to just how the kicker is contacting the ball by the lines they leave on the kicking foot.

The exact spot on which the place kicker's toe should hit the ball is about five inches from the bottom tip of the ball and directly on the rear middle seam.

## 3. PLACE-KICKING PRACTICE DRILL

Use a skeleton unit of a center, holder, place kicker, and two rushers. The rushers line up five yards on either side of the center and alternate rushing the kick on the snap of the ball. It is better to use only one rusher at a time. Also, the rushers should be started from five yards deep in the secondary. This added distance allows for the kick to get off but it is close enough to be a mental factor.

On this drill, you work on the center snap, holder, placement and kick. The timing between these three players is most important. Use at least five balls. A manager or spare player should catch the balls and pass them back to a spare rusher who places the ball by the center. Five minutes a day is sufficient time for this drill.

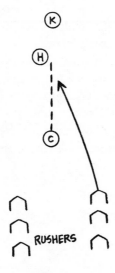

DIAGRAM #175

## 4. FIELD-GOAL DRILL

Use exactly the same setup as in the preceding drill only keep moving the ball back farther and farther. Also, move it from hash to hash. It is a good idea to keep records on successful kicks from the different distances. Not counting the wind factor, you should pretty well know the chances for a successful kick from anywhere from the 40-yard line on in.

## 5. MULTIPLE FIELD-GOAL DRILL

Use your best three field-goal kickers, each with a center and holder. Place the groups in various positions on the field. This drill is designed to save time. Use a stopwatch to time each group. Three to four seconds should be acceptable. Also, you'll need several managers to catch all these balls.

## 6. TEAM RUSH ON EXTRA-POINT ATTEMPTS DRILL

The defensive unit should always rush with at least nine men when trying to block extra-point attempts. There should always be two points of penetration: one from the outside and one up the middle. The reason for not coming from both outsides at once is the injury factor to the rushers. One man will be more reckless when he knows he is not on a collision course with a teammate. The penetration points are areas where you put more rushers than there are blockers. Outside is the more successful, because you can force the offense to block in, avoiding a jammed situation, and spring one man clean. However, this one man is fairly wide by this time. He must get a super start and lay out, stretching his whole body in the air. His arms are outstretched and if he times it right, he has a chance to get his hands on the ball. The middle penetration is a question of finding a crack in the blocking and powering through.

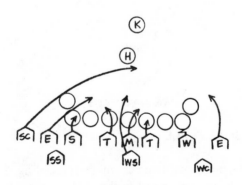

DIAGRAM #176

## 7. TEAM RUSH ON FIELD-GOAL ATTEMPTS DRILL

Rushing field-goal attempts is a different situation because of two reasons. One, there is much more likelihood of a fake field goal and run or pass; and two, you always need a safety to field short kicks. This leaves a maximum front line of eight. Of the eight who line up to rush, two must fake a rush and cover the flats and be containers in the event of a run. You can still try to penetrate at the same two points. The third man in on the left side and the second man in on the right side should draw blocks and then escape into the flat looking for screens or flat passes or a run. The three deep play zone pass defense.

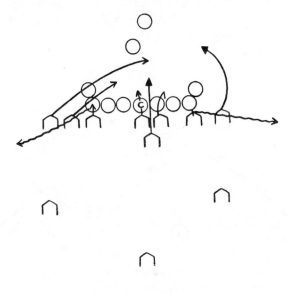

DIAGRAM #177

*Coaching Point:* It is a good idea to have a set return on *all* kicks other than those kicks where a return has been called. Let's take these situations:

1. A punt rush is on.
2. A team comes out on third down and aligns in punt formation.
3. All field-goal attempts.
4. Your opponent quick kicks.

All these situations should have a stock return. Your team will never remember a variety of returns. A good coaching expression is, "All surprise kicks are left returns."

# D. PUNT RUSH DRILL

There are as many punt rushes as there are imaginations to dream them up. From the standpoint of simplicity, it is a good idea to plan your punt return and punt rush from the same front. A couple of exceptions do exist, however. You may want a special rush to take care of a weakness noted in the punt protection of a particular opponent. Also, once in a while, you may want to risk everything and go with a nine- or ten-man rush. Whatever your plan or scheme, this drill is hardly ever done full-speed. You train your players and rehearse the action. Here is a diagram showing a ten-man rush.

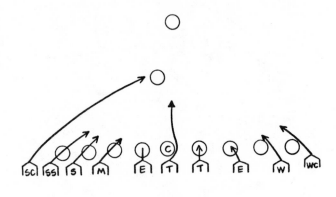

DIAGRAM #178

## E. KICKOFF DRILL

Use the portion of the field between the hashmark and the sideline from far 40-yard line into the goal line. Take your two best kickoff men and place one on the far 40 and one on the goal line. The kicker on the 40 has two footballs and the kicker on the goal line has one already teed up. The kicker on the 40 tees up one ball and kicks it. The kicker on the goal receives the kick while the first kicker tees up his second ball. The receiver then kicks back toward the far 40-yard line. In this fashion each kicker has a teed-up ball waiting. A couple of managers are helpful to field stray kicks. Eight kicks a day are enough. Kickers can swap sides if the wind is a big factor.

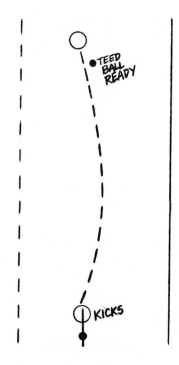

DIAGRAM #179

## F. KICKOFF RETURN DRILL

This is always a team drill. Much time is lost if your kickoff man is a poor one. To make sure the time spent on kickoff returns is meaningful, use a strong passer to simulate the kickoff. This way you can time the reception with the blocking pattern. If your passer can't get the ball high and deep enough, move him 20 yards out in front of the covering team. Like punt returns, you don't want this drill with full-speed blocking. Have the receiving team use a two-arm grab to simulate a block.

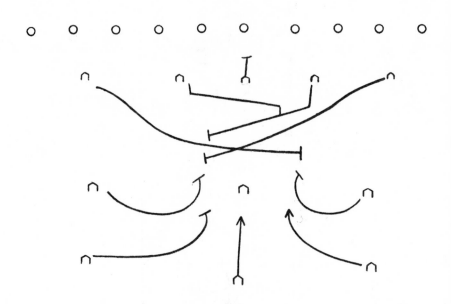

DIAGRAM #180

## G. COMBINATION DRILL

This drill combines centering, kicking, kick rushing, kick coverage, passing and receiving. Use two or three sets of five interior linemen to go one at a time. Also use three kickers in a single file. Set up three sets of defensive ends five yards off the line (this is because there is no blocking for the kicker). Punt receivers are downfield for the reception of the punts.

The sequence works like this: the first set of interior linemen take position; the center snaps to the kicker and the ends rush the kick; the kicker kicks to the punt receivers; the linemen cover in lanes and break down in tackling position when near the punt returner; the punt receiver throws a long pass to one of the linemen who returns the ball to the next center. Offensive ends can also be used if you have enough offensive personnel.

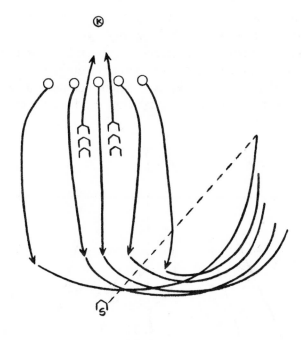

DIAGRAM #181

## H. KICKOFF COVER DRILL

The most dangerous thing you can do is get your 11 fastest men and put them on the kickoff cover team and let them all go for the ball. Kickoffs should be covered in waves. There should be three fast, reckless men who go for the ball, anyway they can get there, as fast as they can get there. The kicker should not be one of these men. It is best to have one next to the kicker and one from each side. The next wave includes everyone but the two safetymen. The second wave tries to stay in lanes and keep containment. Two safetymen back up each side. The ball may be placed anywhere between the hashmarks. It serves the purpose of even spacing if the tee is placed in line with one of the uprights of the goal post. This means you can have a kick coverer five yards from each sideline and exactly five yards apart. This leaves the safetyman and the kicker.

A good way to drill on kickoffs is to start practice with them just as they start the game. Right after warmups, go to four or five kickoff covers, then proceed with the practice schedule. You don't have to have a full receiving team. Kickoff coverage can be timed against the wind. If personnel exist for a scout receiving team, line them up as your next opponent aligns to receive kickoffs. They can form the return, but this should not be done live.

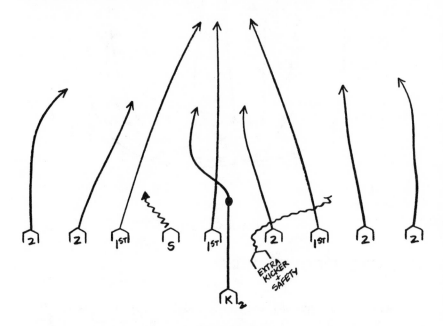

DIAGRAM #182

## I. SURPRISE KICK RETURN DRILL

Your opponent may surprise you with a kick in one of two situations: *one*, it's third down, your opponent has the ball in back of his own 30, the yards remaining may be short or long, your defensive signal caller has called one of your regular defenses, your opponent comes out in punt formation; *two*, your opponent quick kicks. In both cases, you've got to go with the defense called, except your secondary must react. The easiest adjustment is for the strong safety to move to middle safety, the weak safety to retreat to a punt-receiving position and the two corners remain the same. The three secondary men remaining play zone.

Three-deep schemes must rotate back. The best way to drill on this is to have the scout team occasionally pull a surprise kicking situation during your signal drill. Diagram #183 shows a four-deep reaction.

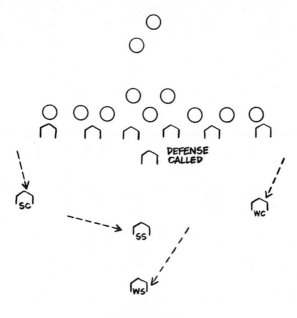

DIAGRAM #183

# 7

# AGILITY, CONDITIONING, AND REACTION DRILLS

## A. AGILITY DRILLS

### 1. MONKEY ROLL

This drill consists of groups of three players. Two players start on their hands and knees and the third is standing. The standing player starts the drill by jumping over the first man positioned on his hands and knees and rolls under the second player. The second player hops over the starting player and rolls under the first man, who was positioned on his hands and knees. He, in turn, jumps and rolls. Each man makes a full body roll after he jumps. As soon as each man rolls, he scrambles to his hands and knees and is ready to jump back over a man rolling into him. In this fashion a constant weave takes place. Ballcarriers should carry footballs when doing this drill.

### 2. BODY ROLL AND JUMP DRILL

Two single lines of players face each other. The first man in each line is given a starting assignment of either jumping over the roller, or rolling under the jumper. The second and third (and so on) men in each line start out by doing the maneuver that is called for; that is, if the man coming at them has just jumped, then they know he follows that by a roll, so they jump over him and then roll themselves. This continues and the two lines gradually draw closer to each other until the rolling and jumping immediately follow each other and the drill becomes a real test of agility.

### 3. CARIOCA

This is a sideways running drill which requires much twisting of the hips. The players form up any number of single lines of five men each. The front men in each line run at the same time for a distance of about 40 yards, and then turn around ready to run back, after the last man in their line has made his run. The carioca is done by facing sideways to the direction of the run. The away foot crosses in front of the leading foot on the first step. The original leading foot never crosses. On the second step the leading foot gains ground forward, straight ahead. On the third step the away foot now crosses behind the leading foot. The process is repeated. To summarize, the leading foot always gains ground by straight steps. The away foot alternates steps in front and then in back. The first attempt at this should be walking and finally build up to running. When players become proficient, races can add to the drill.

### 4. SWITCHING DRILL

This is also a running drill. Players start by facing sideways to the direction of the run. On the starting signal they run back, away from the coach, looking over their shoulder at him. The signal to switch sides is given orally, or by motioning with a football. On this signal, the runners turn while running to face the opposite side. The trick is that they never turn their back to the coach. This requires good balance and short choppy steps with high knee action. All pass defensemen must master this drill.

### 5. CIRCLE RUNNING DRILL

Use the same setup of five men in each line with the leading men in each line running at the same time. On the starting signal, the runners run about half-speed and run in a circle of about five yards in diameter. While running in this circle, they lean to the inside and use good arm action. Gradually they keep tightening up the circle which requires more lean. They try to "get some sand in their hip pocket." By stretching their balance because of the amount of body lean, a player will occasionally slip and fall. Balance can be regained by catching the fall with the inside hand and the running position re-established. On command, all runners sprint out of the circle.

## 6. QUICK-AROUND DRILL

This is similar to the circle run but features only one circle. The players run a straight line to a certain spot. At this point they drop their inside hand to the ground and use it for balance as they run around in one tight circle. After one revolution, they sprint back into a straight line. The idea is to see how quick you can get around the circle and out again.

## 7. CRABBING DRILL

Three men get on their hands and feet in a crabbing position. The coach starts this running drill and either uses voice commands of "right," "left," "forward," "back," or he can use a football to signal direction changes. The players run on their hands and feet using short quick motions. The drill should not be long in duration. You want quickness.

## 8. RUNNING THE SQUARE DRILL

This drill combines several running drills at once. Set up markers, such as towels, hand shields or colored pylons. The markers are in a ten-yard square. The player starts out by sprinting down the first ten-yard leg of the square to the first marker. At this point he does a quick-around around the marker. He then does the carioca the second ten-yard leg of the square. After turning the second marker, he runs backward ten yards and turns the third marker. The last ten yards back to the starting point can be an all-fours crabbing run. A stopwatch will add to the competitiveness of this drill.

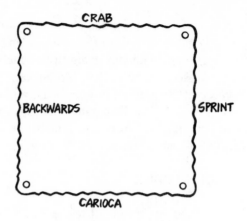

DIAGRAM #184

## 9. TEACHING FORM RUNNING DRILL

This is a drill for the beginners. Young would-be football players seldom really know how to run. Place the players in a circle and have a coach or demonstrator in the middle. All players follow the demonstrator, who goes through the following points: feet apart at shoulder width; lean forward at the waist; both elbows are at the sides of the body with fists clenched; reach out with the right hand as if grabbing an imaginary door handle. Now pull back on the imaginary handle real hard; imagine the door is stuck; as the right arm comes swiftly back, with elbows still close to the side of the body, reach out with the other hand and grab another imaginary door handle. Slowly the procedure is repeated. Reach and pull. The elbows, while close to the sides, go beyond the back at the end of the pull. Tell the trainees to use this arm action, always imagining the handle out in front of them. Next teach footwork. Toes are in and players should have weight on the balls of the feet. Have them step slowly forward landing on the balls of the feet and picking the knees up. Now have them run about half-speed. Stress forward lean, not landing on their heels, and arm action.

## 10. FAKING DRILL

This also is a drill for youngsters. Set up several standing dummies and have players run towards the dummies using good form. When they are several feet away from the dummy, have them plant their right foot and at the same time nod the head and trunk to the right. Then they push off the planted foot back to the left. After all have learned to make a simple fake, have them try a double fake. This involves planting right, nodding right, one more step with left foot which is planting left, and nodding left then breaking back in the direction of the first fake. Experts will make a strong fake on the first step but learn to cut the second fake down so very little time is lost.

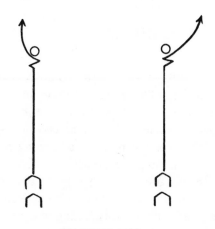

DIAGRAM #185

## QUICK-QUICKS

This is usually a group drill. The leader can do these drills in one of two ways: first, he can make the moves himself and the group must follow; second, he can call out a certain type move, such as side straddle, and the group makes the moves on the command "hike." The idea is to assume a hitting position and make short moves with the arms and hands with an exaggerated quickness. Such common exercises as toe-tapper, sidestraddle, and quarter-eagle are usually used. The exercise is done by the numbers. If the drill is side-straddle, the leader hollers "hike" and everyone slaps his head gear and hops his feet apart and holds for the next "hike." This is a good spirit drill, and is a good way to start off practice.

## ROPES OR TIRES DRILL

Lightweight portable ropes are best for this drill but tires may be used. Players run through the obstacle, planting their feet in the empty spaces. This requires high knee action and nimble feet. There are a number of ways to run through the ropes or tires. One is to run through hitting every hole. Another is to run through hitting every other hole. You can run through sideways, hitting only the holes on one side. The hardest is called the crossover, and on this one the runner crosses his feet from side to side on alternate steps. If old used tires are all you can get, try putting two tires together to make the obstacle higher.

# B. CONDITIONING DRILLS

Conditioning drills should not be confused with warmup drills. Warmup drills consist of loosening and stretching, while conditioning drills extend the stamina. Most any warmup drill can be extended to a point where it becomes a test of stamina. The idea is, however, to use warmup drills solely for the purpose of getting the body ready foi football drills. Conditioning can be achieved from football drills that teach football. In this way you can achieve two objectives at once. However, football today has gotten so complicated that very often teaching has replaced running. It is getting to a point where it is pretty tough to just line up correctly on every play. Therefore, coaches look for a few drills to use at the end of a teaching day that will extend the stamina.

### 1. SPRINT RELAYS

Pair two units, such as one offensive team against one defensive team. Split them up so that half of each team faces the other half at 40 yards' distance. On the starting signal, the first man in each line carries a football to his teammate 40 yards away. After the exchange, the second man races back and so forth.

### 2. LONG-BOMB SPRINTS

Use as many lines and passers as feasible. Have the front men in each line run out for the long bomb. The passers throw high and long.

### 3. BACK AND FORTH

This one will get them tired in a hurry. Take a group of 20 or so players and place them on the goal line. On the command "set" or "down," they assume their stance. On "hike," they sprint ten yards full speed but must stop before the 15-yard line. Don't give them time to blow, but holler "set" or "down" as soon as they turn around. They must assume the stance and right away they sprint back to the goal line. Twenty-five of these will cause much huffing and puffing.

## 4. TEAM SIGNAL DRILL

Line up a full offensive team on the sideline and have them huddle and run a play to the hashmark. They huddle again and run a play back to the sideline. On pass plays, the blockers count five before sprinting to the next line. In a short period of time the whole offense can be run.

## 5. TEAM KICKING DRILLS

These drills are covered in the preceding chapter. They are mentioned here because they are also great for conditioning. Covering or returning punts and kickoffs involve mostly running and can be used at the end of practice where your aim is to have your team leave the field tired.

## 6. WINDSPRINTS

No one likes windsprints but, like death and taxes, they are inevitable. There is no way to make them attractive but you should at least make them fair. Always sprint players in groups of equal speed. Encourage as much competition as you can.

## 7. SITUPS

A good conditioner is to have every player on the squad do 50 situps after sprints. This is the last thing before showers. There is something about situps when you are tired that seems to build up stamina.

## 8. BODY CONDITIONING DRILLS

The previous drills have all been stamina drills. There are many drills to build a stronger body. Every team should have a program of weightlifting and isometrics. It seems that the only time for these drills is during the off season, but a regular time can be worked into the schedule before or after regular practice. The program to be effective must be watched and recorded. Incentive is necessary. That's why recordable weights must be used in conjunction with isometrics. If your school can't afford any equipment, you can still record push-ups, chins, dips, etc. Also, there is one exercise every football player should do daily, and this is neck bridges.

## C. REACTION DRILLS

Many reaction drills appear elsewhere in this book. Such drills as these are covered in detail but here is a quick list:

| | |
|---|---|
| wave drills | reading drills |
| crab drills | one-on-one drills |
| ward-off drills | two-on-one drills |
| ricochet drills | three-on-three drills |
| aping drills | eye-opener drills |
| grass drills | break on ball drills |

This section will deal with conditioning drills that improve reaction. During World War II, these drills were called guerrilla drills. Set the drill up by forming your group into a circle with the coach or exercise leader in the middle. As the group dog trots in the circle, the leader calls out the following exercises:

### 1. CRAB WALK

Players go to all fours and crab forward in the circle. Whistle blows and all return to their feet and continue to dog trot.

### 2. INVERTED CRAB WALK

On signal to exercise, the players go to all fours again but this time they flip over so their backs are to the ground. They proceed in this manner on hands and feet until the whistle.

### 3. BEAR WALK

Again players go to all fours and walk by moving hand and foot on the same side of the body simultaneously. Steps are made by right hand, right foot and then left hand, left foot. Whistle brings them up again.

### 4. ELEPHANT WALK

Players squat while moving forward and drag each hand on the ground. Steps are taken without the hands leaving the ground.

### 5. FORWARD ROLLS

Players, on command, do three or four forward rolls and again, on whistle, return to the dog trot.

### 6. BUNNY HOP

On signal to exercise, players hop forward on both feet at once. Whistle returns them to the dog trot.

### 7. SQUAT JUMPER

At this point, call a halt to the dog trot and have players face to the middle of the circle. Leader calls for squat jumper and demonstrates. Starting position is hands behind head in full squat with feet staggered. On command "exercise," players leap up from full squat to as high in the air as they can jump. They change feet in mid-air so that when they land, the feet are staggered the other way. This is repeated until the whistle blows.

### 8. HAND SLAP PUSH-UPS

Now that the circle is stationary, have players go to the forward leaning rest position for push-ups. Add to the normal push-up by slapping hands at the height of the up movement. After slap, the hands return to normal push-up position and down movement takes place.

### 9. NECK BRIDGES

Players go to flat on their backs. On command "up," they go to full neck-bridge position. Have them rock back and forth. Have them lift one leg while still in the bridge position. Next have them flip over using the top of the head as a pivot. Again they rock back and forth; again have them flip back to the normal bridge position. At whistle they go back to a reclining position.

### 10. NIP-UPS

Following the bridges, the players are on their backs. On command, they place their hands behind their shoulders, roll back with feet in the air, and then thrust and arch their backs, quickly bringing their feet under their body. When done successfully, they should regain their feet this way. Not too many athletes are able to do this all the way, but surprisingly, even the heavier boys can almost do it after a few tries.

### 11. RUSSIAN DANCE

Have each player get a partner from the man closest to him. Having paired off, the players grab hands and go the full squat, but they turn sideways to each other so they can kick forward without hitting each other. By holding at least one hand with their partner, the pair can successfully do the Russian dance. This involves kicking the legs out alternately from the full squat position. After a little practice, most of the players will be able to do the Russian dance without holding on to a partner for balance.

### 12. BOOKENDS

While the players are still grouped as partners, have them stand back-to-back and lock arms. On command "exercise," one of the partners bends forward while the other rocks back and kicks both feet in the air. When the player whose feet were in the air returns back to the ground, he leans forward and the other partner rocks back and kicks his feet in the air. This rocking back and forth requires good balance.

### 13. FIREMAN'S CARRY

Still paired up, the players start this one by having one player jump up on the other's back and locking his legs around his partner's waist and his arms around the other's neck, the carrier grabs his arms around the rider's legs. On command, the carriers start to run in the circle. After a good run, the leader hollers "switch," and the players change position so that both will have been a carrier. Whistle stops the drill.

### 14. INDIAN LEG WRESTLE

Have partners go to ground. They both go to the full reclining position alongside each other. Each has his head at the other's feet. On the starting signal of "go," each player swings his inside leg up and back. They seek to lock legs and make a forward pull. The player who brings the other's body off the ground wins.

### 15. BALANCE GAME

Still grouped as partners, the players square off in front of each other at exactly one arm's length apart. Both hold their hands up in front of their shoulders. The idea is to strike each other using only the hands and striking only the other man's hands. No other part of the body may be used. The loser is the man who moves either foot to regain balance. Reaction is tested because when you see a hand strike coming into your hand, you can give with the blow. This could cause your opponent to lose balance if he has overextended his blow. When both strike at the same time, the hands meet and a great deal of balance is required to maintain balance and not move the feet.

### 16. ROOSTER FIGHT

Partners face each other and grab both arms behind their backs and stand on one foot. At the start of the action, each man goes after the other butting and shouldering while hopping on one foot. The loser is the man who must drop the up-foot in order to regain balance.

## 17. HAND SHIELD FIGHT

Equip each partner with two hand shields. This is a version of the old pillow fight. On the starting signal, let the two partners go at each other with the hand shields. Since both are in football gear, there is no danger of injury.

## 18. FINISHING DRILL

To end these exercises, you want to finish with a running drill. The players are still in a rough circle. Designate one man to get prone on the ground. At the starting signal the circle begins to move toward the prone man. The first player to come to the prone man jumps over him and then flops to a prone position (face down) himself. He should leave about three feet between himself and the first prone man. The next player jumps over the two men, one at a time, and throws himself down. The line continues in this fashion until the last man clears the original man in the prone position. The original man then jumps up and hurdles all the bodies until he comes to the end of the line where he throws himself down again. The whole thing perpetuates itself. Whistle the drill dead when all have had several good sprints.

# 8
# INDOOR DRILLS

Weather can be a big factor in practice plans, so every coaching staff should have a bad-weather plan. Of course, this is defined by the facilities that are available, and since almost every school has a basketball gym, this chapter will be dedicated to drills that can be accomplished in a gym area. There are also some drills for the classroom.

## A. CONDITIONING DRILLS

### 1. CALISTHENICS

Form the team into rows of single file, side-by-side. This will form a large square. The leader faces the group and directs the exercises. Because you are indoors and the rest of the practice will be limited, you will want a heavy dose of exercises. Here is a suggested list of calisthenics for indoors.

#### *Side Straddle Hop*

Start from attention position. On command "exercise," the players swing their arms over their heads and hop their feet a-straddle in one movement. The second movement is back to attention position. This can be done as a four-count exercise by repeating the two movements.

### Toe-Tapper

Start from attention position with feet slightly apart. On starting signal, players bend at the trunk and touch their toes. Second count is to return to upright position and hit the belly with both hands. Third count is to arch and bend the back backward as far as possible while throwing both hands back. The fourth count brings the body back erect and the hands again slap the midsection. The procedure is then repeated.

### Windmill

Starting position is feet a-straddle with both arms outstretched. On the count of one, the players bend and twist the trunk so that the right hand touches the left toe. On the second count they return to the starting position. The third count brings the left hand down to the right toe and on the count of four, the player returns to the starting position.

### Groin Stretcher

Players start from a position of feet spread as wide as possible. Both elbows are bent. On the first count the players bend and stretch, lowering one elbow towards the floor. On successive counts of two and three, they lower the elbow farther each count. On the fourth count, they return elbows back to the starting position. The next set of four counts is done with the other elbow.

### Hamstring Stretcher

Starting position is erect with one leg crossed over the other. On the count of one, the players bend at the waist and extend hands downward toward the toes. On successive counts of two and three, the players bend and stretch a little farther down each time. At the count of four, they all return to the erect position. This is repeated at least five times. They should then cross the other leg over and repeat the exercise.

### Bicycle

Players assume a supine position and then raise the feet in the air until they are over the head. On the command "exercise" the players imitate pedaling a bicycle. After a short and snappy drill, they stop pedaling and scissor their legs. Finally they bend all the way back until the toes touch the floor behind the head.

### Situps

Again from the supine position, players now place both hands behind the head. On command they sit up and rotate the trunk so that the right elbow touches the left knee. On the second count, they return to the supine position. The third and fourth counts repeat the first and second.

### Cannonball

This is started also from the supine position. On the first count, the players rise the upper part of the body to a sitting position. At the same time they bring the knees up to the chest and grasp them in both arms. This requires the body to balance on the end of the spine. On the second count they snap back to the supine position. Counts three and four repeat one and two.

### Can-Can

Lie on the floor in a supine position with arms sideward. Kick right foot to left hand and return. Then kick left foot to right hand and return. Keep the shoulders on the floor and use a twisting movement of trunk and thighs. Repeat four to six times with each leg.

### Rocking Chair

Players lie face down with arms clasped behind the back. Raise upper part of the body off the floor and follow with a rocking motion on the abdomen. By keeping the back arched and alternating raising the upper body with kicking the feet back, a continuous rocking motion is achieved.

### Push-Ups

Players lie, face down, with the palms of the hands on the floor. The back of the hands should be directly under the points of each shoulder. On the count of one, the arms are extended and the body remains rigid. On the count of two, the arms bend back and the body is lowered to a point where the chest barely touches the floor but does not go completely down. Counts three and four repeat.

### Guerrilla Exercises

After a good calisthenics period, the squad can go through all the guerilla exercises as explained in the previous chapter.

### Relays

Indoor running can be made more palatable by forming for relays. There are many types of relays, such as straight sprinting, passing off a football, circling a player or dummy, fireman's carry, etc. The main thing is to get a good dose of running in when you are forced indoors.

## 2. DUMMY DRILLS

These drills should be done in two parts. The first part is to break the squad into their groups with their respective coaches. During this session, coaches work on individual assignments and plans. The second part entails bringing the whole team together. There isn't room in the normal gym for the offensive team to go against a scout team and the defense to do likewise all at the same time. This means the offense must go against the defense in dummy signal drill. Both units will have to sacrifice some, in that both must execute some things that are not in their plans for the benefit of the other. Because of space, the offense cannot run much of a pass drill. However, protection can be checked and routes can be walked through. All phases of the kicking game can be rehearsed without the actual kick.

## 3. CHAIR DRILLS

This is an interesting offensive drill to perfect blocking assignments. It can be done in a classroom, so even if a gym is not available, some good work can be accomplished in bad weather. Also, this is an excellent drill for meeting time. Coaches make the same mistakes most professors make; that is, utilizing too much lecture in classroom time. Players, like students, meet in a small, warm, enclosed area and simply sit and listen—often to a teacher who has a monotone voice and the result is drowsiness. The learning process is speeded up if the students participate. This drill will produce positive learning results.

Take your 11 starting offensive players and place them in their offensive formation. They sit in armless chairs by straddling the chair backwards. Across from them place empty chairs to represent the defense. Use your opponent's defensive alignments. The coach or quarterback calls out the play and quickly hollers "hike." Every player on offense simply points to the empty chair that represents the man he would block on that play. Mistakes are easily discovered. Either two players point to the same chair or one chair doesn't have a "blocker." Hand signals can be developed for faking and pass routes. The drill should be speeded up so there is hardly any thinking time between the play number and the "hike." After the first unit has run through the offense, put the second unit in the chairs and go through the same procedure.

## 4. CLASSROOM DRILLS

### Field-General Drills

Quarterbacks and defensive signal-callers can receive a lot of training in the classroom. They may have to meet in separate rooms with separate coaches, but their training is very similar.

*Voice Drills.* Field generals must practice calling signals. The quality of the voice is important. Clarity is a must. Also the bearing of the caller should be emphasized. The calls should be made with confidence and positiveness. The caller must be a "take charge" guy. He must eliminate extra talking by his teammates. Also, the offensive signal-caller has the added duty of setting the cadence. All your signal-callers should practice cadence calling together with a metronome.

*Recognition Drills.* Both offensive and defensive signal-callers should have instant recognition of what's facing them. Defensive field generals must recognize every offensive set it is possible to line up in, and the offensive caller must instantly be able to call out defensive alignments. Borrowing the old Army training aid of flash cards for aircraft recognition, you can train your callers to have instant recognition. If you happen to have a slide machine, it will be of great value in this drill.

*Situation Drills.* Each signal-caller, either offensive or defensive, can be trained in the classroom to face situations. Blackboard drills are good, but the mock-up field with toy players is better. Not only normal situations can be covered, but change-offs, audibles, and checked defenses can be worked on.

*Field Zones Drill.* Somewhere in the classroom or locker room you should have a large diagram of a football field showing the zones of the field. These zones have changed over the years. Today the third-down punt is a rarity but there was a time when the field could be zoned by downs. From the goal to the 30 used to be two-down zone. From the 30 to the opponent's 40 was three-down zone. From there on it was four-down zone. Each zone had a certain type of offense connected with it. The same is still true today even if most teams wait until fourth down to punt. Here is another sample of zone strategy.

*1. From your goal to your own 10*–Run the same offense you would run from opponent's 8 to opponent's goal line. In other words, run your goal-line offense. Of course, you would punt on fourth down.

*2. From your 10 to your 40*–Use basic run plays. Do not risk multiple ball-handling. Don't throw in the middle or cross-field throwbacks.

*3. From your 40 to opponent's 40*–Run just about the whole offense but eliminate high risk scoring plays.

*4. From opponent's 40 to opponent's 8*–Everything goes. Fourth down used for first-down attempt or field-goal attempt.

*5. From opponent's 8 to the goal*–Use your goal-line offense.

### Film Drills

These are for the whole squad. Nowadays most films are made up with the offense and defense broken down. The first drill on films comes with studying your own films. Each coach must meet with his group to go over every scrimmage and game film. It is essential that positive things are pointed out as well as negative things. Players can learn from both. The second drill is with your opponent's films. The first time or two let the players just watch to get an overall feeling. After that you want to tie-in the scouting report on tendencies, field position, hash reaction, etc. Finally, use the film to have the callers call defenses (or plays) and then study how that would have gone versus the play that came up next. Also, there is value in having the players come by on their own to study their own positions. A really concerned and motivated player can often find little things the staff may have missed.

### Written Tests Drills

During early season, everyone on the team should be given written tests on assignments and responsibilities. This is not only for the pupil, but it shows the staff where the instruction has fallen down. After the season gets underway, there should be a scouting report test at the end of the week. It's not a bad idea to give such test on Friday (if game is on Saturday). If the game requires travel to get to the game site, give the test en route.

### Chart Drills

Both offense and defense should keep running charts throughout the season. The offense wants to chart each play at the point of attack, and each pass attempt. Records show how many times, average gain, etc. The defense does the same, which shows breakdowns on each defense. These charts can go as far as the imagination and time available to prepare them. Many teams have managers or graduate assistants to do this work. The results are posted each week where the players involved can study them. Conclusions should be apparent and coaches should confer with players about the results.

# 9

# TEN TOP DRILLS
# OF THE
# LAST DECADE

Choosing the ten top drills of the last ten years is a tall order. The final criterion in the selection of these drills was based on which drills could least be done without. A balance was sought so that the drills would cover all aspects of football. Here then are ten drills that every football team should have in its repertoire.

First, the complete list, following which is a description of each drill.

| *Drill* | *Who For* |
|---|---|
| 1. Hamburger or Oklahoma | Everyone |
| 2. 3-on-3 with Backs | Offensive Line |
| 3. Burma Road and Score | Offensive Backs |
| 4. Live Dummy Team Drill | Offensive & Defensive Teams |
| 5. Eye-Opener | Defensive Linebackers |
| 6. Zone Position Drill | Defensive Secondary |
| 7. Keying (or Reading Drill) | Defensive Front Seven |

## DRILL NO. 1: HAMBURGER OR OKLAHOMA DRILL

This drill features all the techniques of offensive line blocking, defensive hit, escape and tackle, quarterback handoff and ballcarrying. By using five of these drills at once, every position on offense and defense can be worked on the fundamentals of their position. The following description encompasses one complete drill.

Place two markers on the ground exactly seven feet apart. The drill can be executed with almost any kind of marker, but if you really want to keep the running back in the hole, use two standing dummies with holders. Place one offensive blocker between the two markers. His hands should be even with the back edge of the marker. Across from him place a defensive man. The defensive man must keep at least the width of the ball between himself and the blocker, but he can align as far back as two yards. When a quarterback and center are available, they are placed away from the hole created by the markers in such a way that the quarterback can make a handoff to a running back right behind the blocker. The drill can be run without a center or quarterback. Simply give the running back a ball before the play starts. The running back should not be more than three yards from the line of scrimmage. If you use a center and quarterback, the play starts in a normal manner, if not, when everyone is in position, the play starts with a "hike" by the coach. The offensive blocker fires out and tries to knock the defender out of the hole and maintain pressure on him so that he cannot escape for the tackle. The defender hits the blocker and tries to keep him from getting into his body. While holding off the blocker, he tries to determine the path of the ball and attempts to get into tackling position and then makes the tackle, if possible. The ballcarrier runs straight at the back of the blocker and breaks between the markers on the block of the offensive blocker.

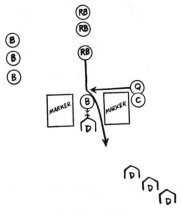

**DIAGRAM #186**

## DRILL NO. 2: 3-ON-3 WITH BACKS

This drill is listed for offensive linemen, but it is also excellent for offensive backs and can be used for defensive linemen as well. It is, however, the best drill for offensive linemen there is.

Align three offensive linemen across the field in the following manner: put one on the vertical five-yard line stripe facing across the field rather than down the field; the other two align even with the first but only half-way to the next five-yard line. You now have three blockers exactly 2½ yards apart. Behind them set up three running backs. The use of a quarterback is optional, but if the middle blocker is a center with a quarterback behind, the backs get more out of the drill. The backs and three blockers huddle for designation of a point of attack. When the action starts, the backs run a handoff or sweep at the various possible places across the length of the three blockers. In front of each blocker, place a full-speed defender. Each play features one blocker who is at the point of attack and two who must make cutoff blocks. The backs never block. They run straight handoffs or wide. If defense is also being taught at the same time, the sweep must be restricted by a dummy inside of which the ballcarrier must run.

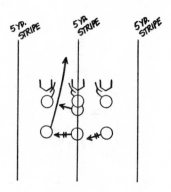

DIAGRAM #187

## DRILL NO. 3: BURMA ROAD AND SCORE

There are many types of Burma Road drills, but to get the most out of the drill in teaching backs to run, there should be the following features: a handoff reception, a jump or leap over an obstacle on the ground, several direction changes featuring butt-offs, pivots and straight-arms and, finally, a drive between two standing dummies (or defensive players) to score. The drill should always end in a score.

A line of backs position to receive the handoff one at a time. Each back runs the ''Burma Road'' as described above. This drill teaches most of the skills of ballcarrying.

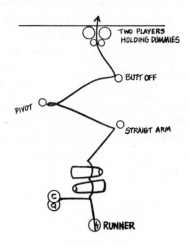

DIAGRAM #188

## DRILL NO. 4: LIVE DUMMY TEAM DRILL

Either offense or defense must have a full-speed drill without the risk of too many injuries. The idea is to time-out the play with all blocking full-speed and all defensive reaction full-speed but eliminate tackling and the pileups that always come in scrimmage. Another name for this drill is "butt-off." The term means the defense butts the ballcarrier but does not tackle him. It is almost impossible to do this drill with the number one offense against the number one defense, but it is excellent versus scout teams or the JVs. There is enough reaction to make the drill realistic but not enough to be a hairy dog fight. The defense absolutely cannot do without this drill during the season. The offense will find the drill far superior to running the bags.

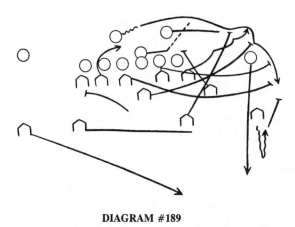

DIAGRAM #189

## DRILL NO. 5: EYE-OPENER

This is classified as a linebacker drill, but is also excellent for all defensive personnel. This is the best tackling drill there is. Place four markers on the field two yards apart. The markers may be hand shields, rubber pylons, tall dummies laid down or even towels. Place a line of defensive players even with the first marker and one yard behind it. Players come to the front position one at a time. Next, place a line of ballcarriers two yards away from the first marker and two yards deep. They also come up one at a time. The drill is ready to start when ballcarrier and first defensive man are in position. On command "hike," the ballcarrier heads for the holes made by the markers. He may break fast and hit one hole full-speed, or he may fake several holes before choosing one. The defensive player shuffles across the holes, on his side of the markers, keeping tackling leverage on the ballcarrier.

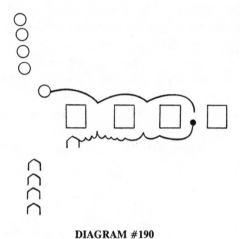

DIAGRAM #190

## DRILL NO. 6: ZONE POSITION DRILL

The most difficult thing in teaching zone defense is to get all seven defenders in the middle of their zones. The reason this is difficult is because zone sizes change according to lateral position across the field from hashmark to hashmark. Zone sizes are also affected by rotation. An example of this would be a weak rotation into the sidelines. Even though unlikely, it could happen. This means the strong linebacker has a flat ten yards deep and all the way across the field to the far sideline. First he has to read pass and then sprint like a maniac to get into his zone. In fact, on passing situations, he has to cheat on alignment to get there in time. This is probably the toughest example, but every down features a difference, no matter how subtle. Even the action of the ball can change zone position.

Place a quarterback with a football on one hashmark. Have a full seven-man secondary facing him in their normal positions. Declare a strong formation either to the field or to the boundary. Linebackers and safeties align accordingly. Rotation can be pre-called or is now called because of the strength factor. No matter what, the rotation is either to or away from the boundary. Have the quarterback holler ''hike'' and take an imaginary snap and then set up straight back or pull up right or left, or sprint right or left. After the quarterback reaches passing position, the coach blows a whistle and all action stops. The coach now checks each defender to see if his position is such that all areas overlap. The drill stays on this hash until all possible combinations have been covered. Then the ball is moved to the center of the field and everything is repeated. Finally, the ball is moved to the remaining hash and the drill is again repeated. Versus sprintouts, defenders must learn to drift with the ball, always keeping relative spacing with each other and the boundary.

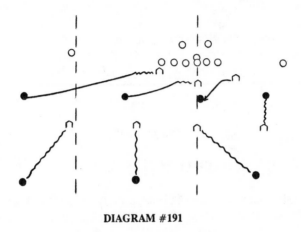

DIAGRAM #191

## DRILL NO. 7: KEYING OR READING DRILL

Defensive linemen and linebackers must spend the majority of their time learning to play the base defense. This is always a keying or reading defense. Young linemen find this difficult and experienced linemen need to keep sharp. This drill should be done every day.

The defensive line coach gets seven JV linemen as a line of scrimmage. In front of them he places his first defensive line. He gets behind one of the defensive linemen and hand signals to the offensive blockers involved in blocking that one man. On "set," the whole offensive line takes their stances but on "hike," only the key blocker, or blockers, block on the man in front of the coach. This means the defender must react to reach, turnout, double-team, fireout, pass, and trap blocks. After that particular blocker has had a variety of different blocks, the coach moves over behind another defender and the same process is repeated until all four have "read" all types of full-speed blocks. It may seem that some time is wasted because only one man is "live" while three others are just waiting, but when the offensive blockers understand the drill and hand signals, it can go very fast. There is no huddle and the blocks come just as fast as the offense can realign.

COACH GIVES HAND
SIGNALS TO "ALIVE" BLOCKERS
AND TYPE BLOCK TO USE.

DIAGRAM #192

## DRILL NO. 8: COUNTY FAIR

Nothing can beat the County Fair for conditioning the greatest number in the shortest time. The drill can be done either before regular practice, or after, or both.

Set up stations around the practice field with a coach at each station. Line up the entire squad in groups of anywhere from five to ten players. Send out one group at a time. They sprint to the first station. Each station features a good tough physical activity. As the first group finishes the first station, they sprint to the second and the next group then sprints to the first station. The procedure continues until the last group finishes the last station. There is no firm criterion as to what each station ought to be but here is a sample list.

Station   1—Monkey rolls
Station   2—Wave drill
Station   3—Ropes
Station   4—Zig-zag run
Station   5—Fumble recovery
Station   6—Play the piano on the big sled
Station   7—Circle run
Station   8—Carioca run
Station   9—Tackling dummy
Station 10—Fireman's carry

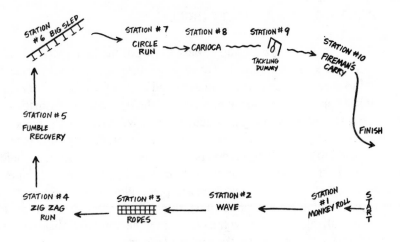

DIAGRAM #193

## DRILL NO. 9: RUN THE SQUARE

There are many agility drills, some of which are or can be included in Drill No. 8. But if you want one drill that best tests the ability to coordinate the body, it would have to be running the square.

Get four rubber pylons and place them at the four corners of a ten-yard leg; use the portable ropes, or use old tires if ropes are not available. Start players out one at a time running the first leg. As the first player clears the ropes (or tires), he immediately runs the carioca down the second leg and rounds the pylon. The third leg can be the backward run and when he rounds the third pylon, he crabs the last ten yards. This 40-yard obstacle run can be run against a stopwatch.

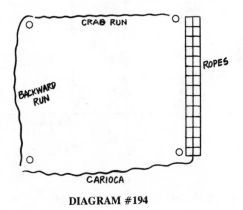

DIAGRAM #194

## DRILL NO. 10: SPECIALTY DRILL

This is a kicking drill and it best utilizes time and space for all phases of the kicking game. First, all specialists should warm up and then go to special areas of the field assigned to them. Place kickers and holders and one center go to the north end of the field and use from the 40 to the goal for place-kicking practice. Kickers will need a ball shagger. The other 60 yards of the field is used by the punters. A couple of centers are assigned to them. Punt receivers line up at the 10-yard line to field punts. Kickoff men split up on the sidelines and kickoff to each other. Centers rotate between punting area and place-kicking area. Specialists can report to practice early and finish this drill in about 20 minutes. If your squad all takes the field at the same time, the non-specialists should go to their respective coaches for a relaxed coverage of personal areas of weakness such as pulling, etc. This is also a good time to have the defensive front seven run through their blitzes against the posts. At the end of specialty period, the whole team should come together for team calisthenics, and practice has now started.

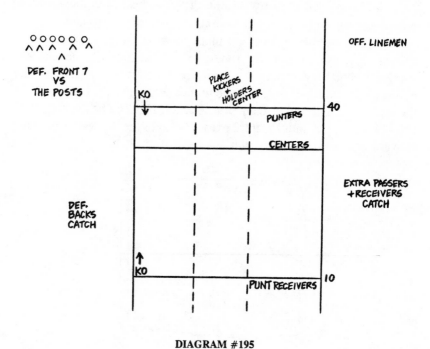

**DIAGRAM #195**

# INDEX